TYPO-
GRAPHY
SKETCH-
BOOKS

D1340920

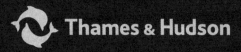

TYPO-GRAPHY SKETCH-BOOKS

STEVEN HELLER & LITA TALARICO

With over 600 illustrations

CONTENTS

ALL LETTERS, ALL THE TIME.

STEVEN HELLER
& LITA TALARICO

Every designer, regardless of race, creed or nationality, understands the language of type. A graphic designer who is not fluent is not a graphic designer.

In Steven Spielberg's *Close Encounters of the Third Kind*, aliens communicate to humans through mathematics. One could argue that type is the mathematics of graphic design. Designers (who are sometimes considered alien) share their passions through type. Not all designers can understand what is communicated through Roman, Arabic or Cyrillic scripts, but they can embrace all letters in the abstract and intuit intent.

When playing with or caressing type, it is not so much what it says, or in what specific tongue a message is communicated that matters most. An understanding of content and context is essential, but, typographically speaking – that is, in terms of the letterforms – beauty, however defined, is key. The beauty of precision; the beauty of expression; the beauty of how one letter conjoins with others on either side of it and above and below; the beauty of how it looks on page or screen. Alas, unlike mathematics, which is presumably the *lingua franca* of interplanetary life forms, type probably will not translate well on other stars, moons and planets, but it is certainly what joins diverse designers together through common passion.

There are two kinds of type maker (though many more kinds of type user, which is another story). One is the precisionist or functional designer who creates typefaces for quotidian public consumption. The other is the gadfly or expressionist designer who makes – or, rather, illustrates – letters in any shape or form: legible or illegible, it doesn't matter, as long as it emotes. In the process of assembling this collection of typographic sketchbooks we sought out both kinds of maker (since all graphic designers are also users, users were not the targeted segment). It was fairly obvious from their responses which individuals did what kind of type design. Even these personal books and scraps that were never meant to be seen in public revealed the discipline, or lack of it, that defines the designers' practices.

Masters of functional design, such as Matthew Carter, Erik Spiekermann and James Montalbano, never really let their hair down. They showed their resolute precision even in the most informal contexts. But functional purity is not limited to veteran type designers. Look at Tom Geismar's roughs for logos or Oded Ezer's Hebrew lettering to find sketches that could easily be used as finishes. Even hand-lettering mavens such as Niels Shoe Meulman are careful not to make a misstep even in sketch form.

Yet sketchbooks are intentionally informal – a place to rehearse, experiment or just play around. The vast majority of pages selected for this book are indeed typographic playgrounds, where anything from doodles to noodles to more ambitious renderings are nurtured and stored. For the most part the type is the main focus, as in Leigh Wells's notations of vintage signs. But illustrations such as Tom Schamp's delightful anthropomorphic letters are also included. Sometimes sketchbooks reveal the progress of assignments, as ideas are developed. Others are wonderfully random musings (in print and on printouts from the screen), like Pedro Inoue's drawn and constructed concoctions. In many instances they are novel approaches that lean more towards fine than applied art, as with Aleksandar Maćašev's Moleskine books filled with a wide array of drawings, paintings and cuttings. Pierre di Sciullo says a sketch can "sometimes be viewed for itself, not like a former step of something else."

The designers here agree that their sketchbooks are *aide-mémoires* for ideas that would otherwise be forgotten, but we view these type sketchbooks as having one key thing in common: they are personal narratives, not conventional stories but tales about form and content. Through sketched and finished letterforms we see how type designers and typographers address the vessel in which meaning is contained. While many of these alphabets are designed to be neutral, many more are meant to be demonstrative – not only to aid a story but also to fill in the gaps. As Ovidiu Hrin notes:

"These books help me very much with a clear overview and insight into my past self. Every now and then I take one or two days off and take every journal, almost page by page, to see who I was, what I was thinking and how everything relates to this moment I've created for myself."

Reza Abedini

Tehran, Iran-born designer Reza Abedini, the founder in 1993 of Reza Abedini Studio, still retains some of his sketches from twenty-two years ago when he was at art school. "They were various random sketches and I put them together afterwards," he recalls. "Some years later I realized that I need to have a notebook with me all the time to write down or draw my ideas more professionally."

He is no longer living in the Iranian capital. "We moved to the Netherlands almost two years ago and I'm working in Amsterdam, but still I'm doing different projects in my own country. For example, I'm editor-in-chief of a magazine on the Persian writing system, language and typography." Type is clearly extremely important to him.

In the beginning, Abedini notes, "sketching was just for saving the ideas which were coming to my mind without any exact subject. For example, most of the time when I'm reading Persian classical literature I get many ideas for typography. So I need to save them, because they are based on the poem that I have read at the time – almost like improvisation. I now have different sketchbooks (or ideas books) and they contain combinations of writing, drawings, and visual notes on typography, type design, ceramics, poetry, and design."

Diego Giovanni Bermúdez Aguirre

Born in Cali, Valle del Cauca, Colombia, graphic and type designer Diego Giovanni Bermúdez Aguirre is a professor at Javeriana University and consultant to the program "Bogotá Innova" (Chamber of Commerce of Bogotá). His work reflects the vibrancy and color of his native Colombia, while hinting at a psychedelic past.

He has archived his sketches since 1994 when he was studying at the Universidad Nacional de Colombia, where he received his degree in graphic design. About his ad-hoc output he notes in a poetic cadence, "My sketches are done to define and clarify my doubts, to realize my ideas." He adds, "The sketches are performed in order to reflect and explore different options for each communication."

Aguirre's sketches are very expressive, but he later seeks to "realize them in the computer. They are the prelude to the final result, but sometimes I prefer the sketches to the outcome!" He almost never uses photographic images in his design or sketchbooks because "I try to work with very basic typographic and graphic elements."

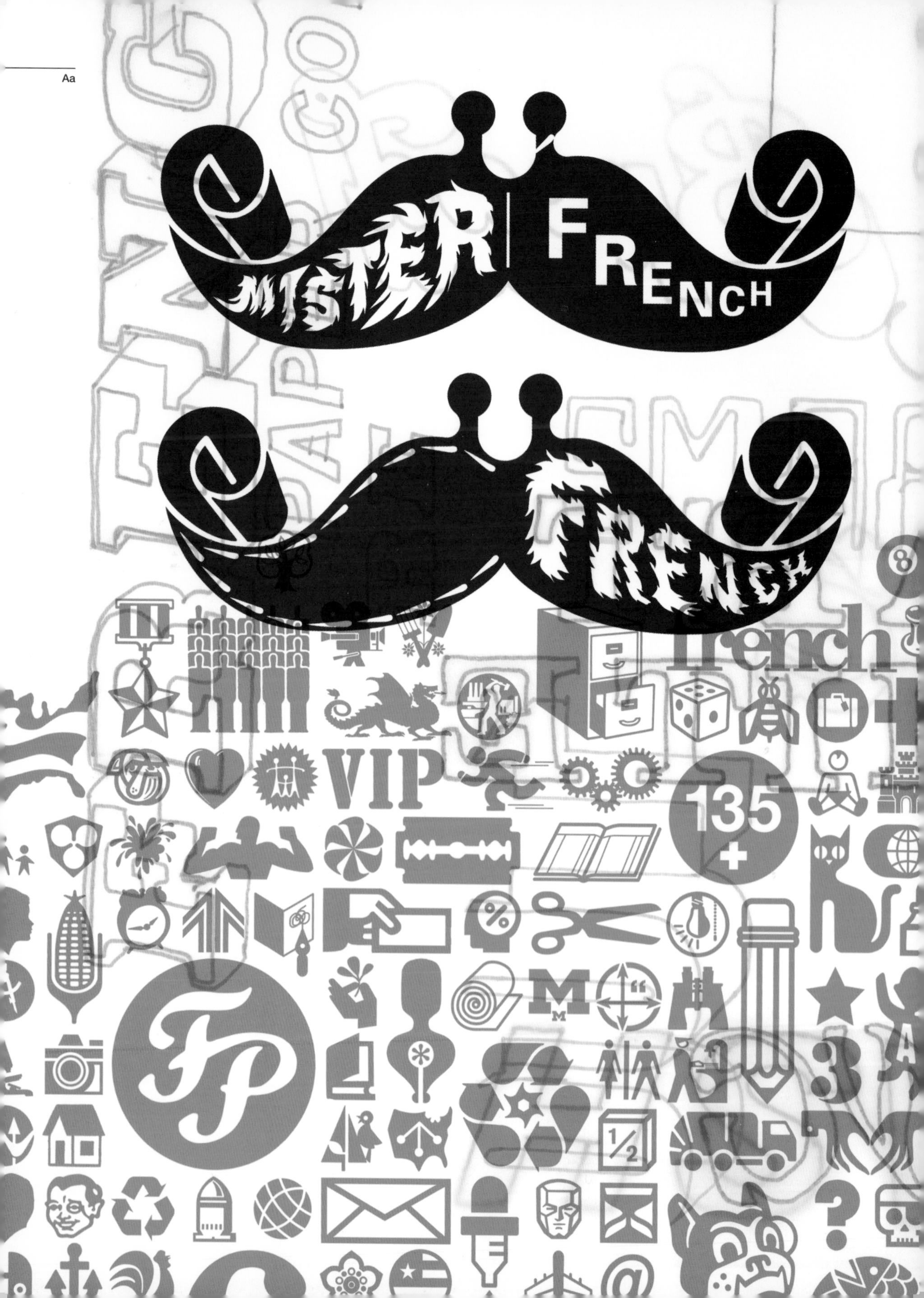
MISTER FRENCH
FRENCH
french
VIP
135

The french paper co.

Charles Spencer Anderson

Minneapolis-based designer and design entrepreneur Charles Spencer Anderson runs his CSA studio where, he claims, "Most of our designers have used sketchbooks since high-school age." The books generally have a focused function, he says: "Many of these sketches are ideas that get abandoned as the thinking or project gets more refined." Of course, there's a certain spontaneity – even to sketches done on the computer – where the designer gets lost in minute details and individual elements (as opposed to the overall design of a piece). "It's often refreshing to look back at sketches for the unintended and unpredictable parts, then take them on their own merits," he adds.

The CSA studio creates many time-intensive campaigns and promotions for longstanding clients, such as French Paper. "French Paper pieces, including swatch books, have to stay relevant for several years because the paper lines are difficult to change, and because they don't have huge printing budgets like some of their competitors." So, Anderson explains, "We are constantly reinventing the look and message within the pre-existing parameters determined by their product. The sketches are often design work that falls between the cracks of our process – but they are a great short-hand of our inspirations and improvisations."

13

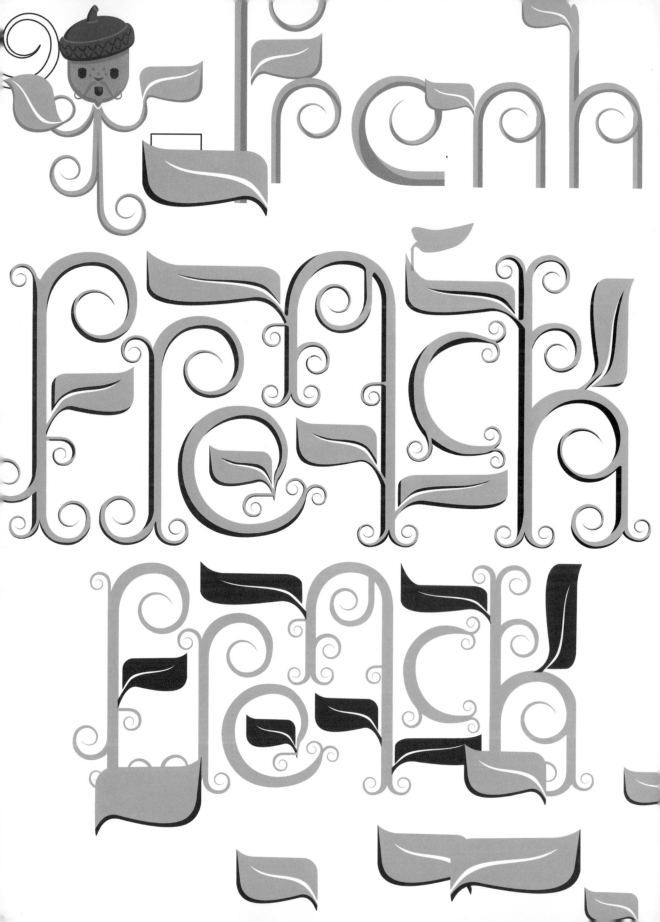

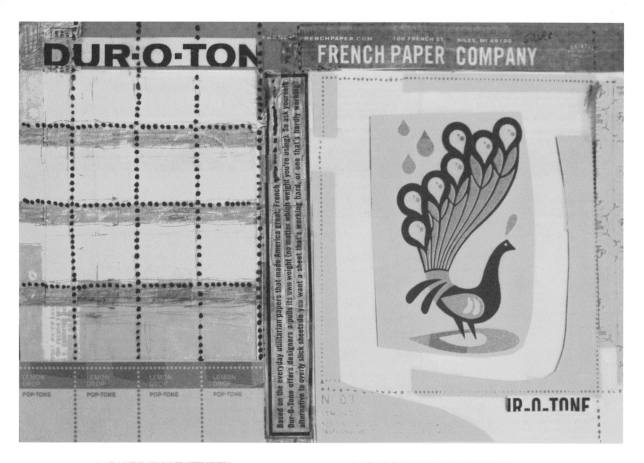

DUR-O-TONE

FRENCH PAPER COMPANY

Based on the everyday utilitarian papers that made America great, French Dur-O-Tone offers designers a pull its own weight (no matter what weight you're using). So ask yourself alternative to overly slick sheets do you want a sheet that's working hard, or one that's hardly working

IR-O-TONE

LEMON DROP   LEMON DROP   LEMON DROP   LEMON DROP
POP-TONE   POP-TONE   POP-TONE   POP-TONE

RECYCLING NATURE'S TEARS SINCE 1922

100%
HYDROPOWER

SPECKLETONE ‣ DUR-O-TONE POP-TONE
MOD-TONE ‣ PARCHTONE ‣ SMART WHITE
CONSTRUCTION ‣ MUSCLETONE

100%
HYDROPOWER
FRENCH PAPER CO

Susan Archie

Atlanta, Georgia-based illustrative letterer Susan Archie says that sketching was one of the things her mother would do with her. "Mostly portraits, horses, and roses," she recalls. "When I got older I would sketch things I found in album covers. Elton John's *Goodbye Yellow Brick Road* was illustrated with drawings that mesmerized me, and I copied them all into my own books. I quit drawing in art school because I really wasn't any good compared with others. I started writing in spiral-bound or case-bound blank books and taking photos instead."

Archie uses "sketches" to help her find the right typeface for a project. "I look in my font books, through my font collections, and/or online, then I set my choices and whittle down. What looks good in books or online doesn't necessarily look good as brand – sometimes there are weird letter details that don't look right. This method helps me analyze and compare very quickly," she says. Oddly, she laments not drawing for fun any more. "I 'sketch' concepts in Photoshop or Illustrator and try to get sparks flying. My creative time is usually after dark when I've had time to relax. I try to let go – make mistakes, use the wrong color – so that my innate 'control' gene relaxes and allows possibilities to happen."

THE RED FOX CHASERS

THE RED FOX CHASERS

THE RED FOX CHASERS

THE RED FOX CHASERS

I'M GOING DOWN TO NORTH CAROLINA:
THE **R**ED **FOX** CHASERS
The Complete Recordings
[1928–31]

I'M GOING DOWN TO NORTH CAROLINA:
The Complete Recordings of
THE **R**ED **FOX**
CHA**S**ERS
[1928–31]

I'M GOING DOWN TO NORTH CAROLINA:
The Complete Recordings of The Red Fox Chasers [1928–31]

I'M GOING DOWN TO NORTH CAROLINA:
The Complete Recordings of The Red Fox Chasers [1928–31]

**I'M GOING DOWN
TO NORTH CAROLINA:**
The Complete
Recordings of
The Red Fox Chasers
[1928–31]

**I'M GOING DOWN
TO NORTH CAROLINA:**
The Complete
Recordings of
The Red Fox Chasers
[1928–31]

**I'M GOING DOWN
TO NORTH CAROLINA:**
The Complete
Recordings of
The Red Fox Chasers
[1928–31]

Aa

Dmitri Aske

Dmitri Aske, of Sicksystems in Moscow, started sketching in 2000 when he got interested in graffiti. For six years he made sketches on A4 sheets of paper and kept them in folders. Since 2006 he has been using a sketchbook, "because it's much more convenient," he explains.

Aske used to sketch a lot more: "I would make sketches with pencil, pen, and markers just for the sake of the process, and also to develop my style. Those were sketches that could have been turned into graffiti pieces. Today I make only pencil sketches for vector illustrations or other projects I'm working on."

He admits that sometimes his sketches (these are from 2007 to 2010) look fresher than the finished works, "because the lines are less precise than those of the computer images. Sketches definitely have their own charm. Not long ago nearly all my sketches and finished works were based on letters and typography. However, I'm always trying to move forward and develop my art, so now I'm experimenting a lot with people's faces and abstract forms."

Bob Aufuldish

Bob Aufuldish designs typefaces from his studio in San Anselmo, California. These sketches (ranging from the 1990s to 2009) are created for his personal pleasure. "They point in a direction I might pursue for a project some day, or maybe not," he says.

Some of these are actual working sketches for a typeface called Turrell (opposite). "I cut letters as small as possible looking through a loupe using an X-Acto knife. It was an attempt to de-skill myself," he explains. For another exercise he found a stick that looked like a leaping figure and "I saved the stick for years, thinking that someday I could use it for something."

He's also had his way with other flora, what he calls "type flowers." "These are the raw scans of letters I made out of artificial flowers for a poster for an architecture lecture series. Unlike everything else I sent, these have an actual purpose in the final piece. We have an old oversize SCSI scanner here that has an enormous depth of field that's perfect for scanner photos," he explains.

If there is one word to categorize the majority of his books, he says, it would be "prelude."

? ? @

? 1 2 5 7 8 9 . , !

3 6 *

J M Y W X Z

K K (| K

→ O BART É' UM CARA MANEIRO.
(O ESQUEMA DA BIKE FOI PERFEI
TO POIS PASSEI EM LUGARES QUE NUN
CA PASSARIA DE 'ÔNIBUS OU TRAM...
FOI MUITO BOA A REUNIÃO... (COMO
UMA PESSOA PODE SER
TÃO BOM, QUE NÃO CON
SEGUE TRA
BALHO?)
IMPOSSÍVEL...
DE FATO...
POSSO ME
FOI E ESTÁ'
ADPTAR...
SENDO UM DIA
PARA
EXCELENTE
DESENVOL
PORQUE
VER PRO
RESOLVI
JETOS
PENDÊNCIAS
PARA
FIZ CONTATOS,
PROUD
VI A'DAM...
FOI NA (180)
VI AMIGOS.
ACHO QUE AINDA VOU
VER O CHINA EM R'DAM...
SUPER COOL! SUPER MESMO! JANTAR?
ESTOU NO TREM INDO PARA R'DAM
VOU PARA O ESTÚDIO.
(AINDA DEI MEU LUGAR NO TREM
PARA UMA SENHORA)

HOJE FINALMENTE DEVOLVI A BIKE
PARA O MARK, FINALMENTE...
(PROUD!)
FUI LÁ, PROCUREI,
ACHEI, ENCHI O
PNEU! AVI DE BIKE
ATÉ A CASA DO
DONALD... PA
RA APRENDER
O SOFTWARE DE
SOM, PARA EDITAR
AS ENTREVISTAS
DO TYPERADIO...
FOI MUITO LE-
GAL TER ENTRA
DO UM POUCO
NA VIDA DELES...
O CARA MORA DEN
TRO DE UM BAR
CO... IMPRES
SIONANTE...
FOI MUITO
LEGAL. NÃO É
MUITO COMPLEXO NÃO, TEM QUE TER
ATENÇÃO... COMI COM ELE UM PASSINHO
ANTES' DE SEGUIR PARA A PROUD DESI
GN... ACHO QUE CAMELEI TODO O SOUTH
DE AMSTERDAM ANTES DE CHEGAR LÁ...

---

09 - 01 - 10
Realmente fiquei bem proud com
o resultado do Novo Trabalho...
... não esperava... ficou perfeito.
Posso expandir a partir desse
modelo. Seguir desenvolvendo
Caligrafia e tipografia para
instalações e "ESCULTURAS".
Preciso encontrar uma forma
de manter isso alive... pensar
em uma estratégia para mos
Trar esse trabalho para NANZU
KA FIRST. Depois DK... Sweden
Começar! Acho que encontrei
o que estava em busca...
ART + TYPE + CALLIGRAFIA +
DESIGN. USAR como promo
máximo e absoluto. E pensar
em Novas frases 2 palavras...
continuar Postais e LASER.
(no avião) neva bastante...
nunca fiz um take off na
neve, vai ser maneiro.

PROMO

SITES
UPDATES.

FOTOGRAFAR
CAIXA.

QUEM?
1. NANZUKA.
2. ROJO ART SPACE
NYC
3. ZAKKA
4. DUTCH GUYS
SILO/DC/...
5. MAXALOT
6. OTHER
SPACES
7. COLLETE
PARIS
8. BERLIN
9. GLASS
WORKS.
10. VENDER!

3 EXPOSIÇÕES NO
ANO? BCN / NY / JP / A'dam

LINKADA

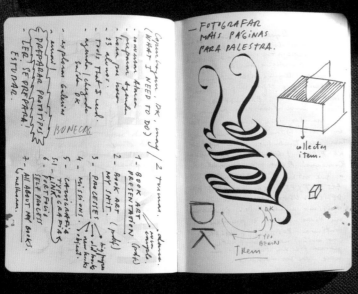

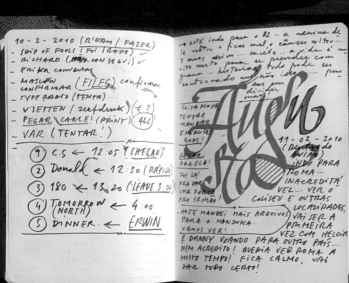

Yomar Augusto

Yomar Augusto was born in Brasilia, raised in Rio de Janeiro, and trained as a graphic designer before going on to study photography at the School of Visual Arts in New York. Since 2002 he has been running experimental calligraphy workshops in Brazil, Russia, Portugal, and the Netherlands, where he now lives. He is also part of the Rotterdam Collective.

He calls his sketchbooks "my studio inside my backpack" where he stores ideas and processes. "I never throw away anything," he notes. "Design is a profession attached to waste, so the sketchbooks are great to keep this 'waste.' My sister is an art bookbinder, so my life is just perfect! Just think or dream about any book, and puff!"

Augusto adds that these books are "sometimes just a place for a creative person to put twelve hours of bad day work on the paper, without any restriction or taste. You are finally free of the 'glare' of the design world and that's the space. Do it. Use it. Nobody is watching. There's no 'cool,' 'great,' 'nice,' or 'awesome.' They are just words. I do calligraphy, so sketchbooks are the perfect platform to be 'ugly,' 'uncool,' 'unwise' and 'unattractive.'"

27

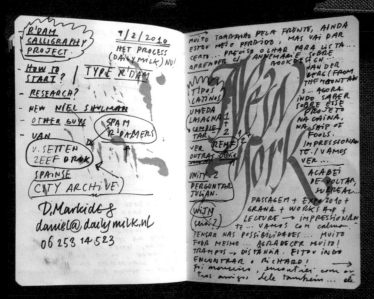

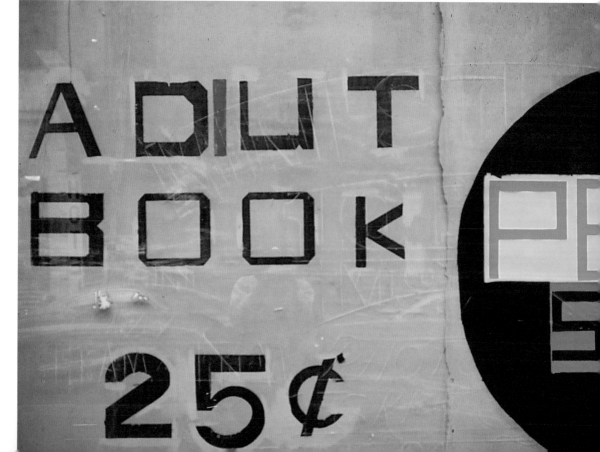

John Baeder

Nashville, Tennessee-based painter and roadside maven John Baeder has been collecting primitive signs or graphic folk art for decades. "I don't keep sketchbooks in the classic sense of drawings, as most of us had to do in art school," he reports. Instead he has kept photo "sketchbooks" or visual notes "of anything that attracts my eye." In the beginning, "there was no purpose, everything was for my own personal pleasure." The sign photographs eventually evolved into an article in *Print* magazine in January 1971. Years later, Abrams published Baeder's *Sign Language: Street Signs as Folk Art* (1996).

Baeder's finished works are totally different from these signs. They are paintings of early diners and other roadside culinary eccentricities. "However, when signs appear, I play the role of a sign painter, or the anonymous person who needs to express themselves with the written word," he says. In other words, he paints signs.

His passion is for exploring "how folks take a writing instrument and apply paint or other materials to communicate myriad thoughts and ideas on a surface. It usually goes unnoticed, how letterforms take on varying personalities from untrained eyes, and how this expression becomes another art form. What I label the 'music of the street.'"

The theme of these collections is "the human spirit, and the need to communicate through the written word."

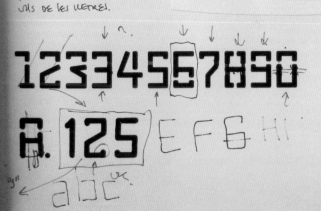

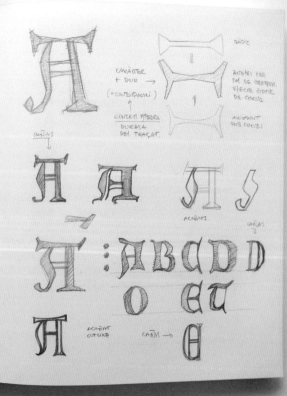

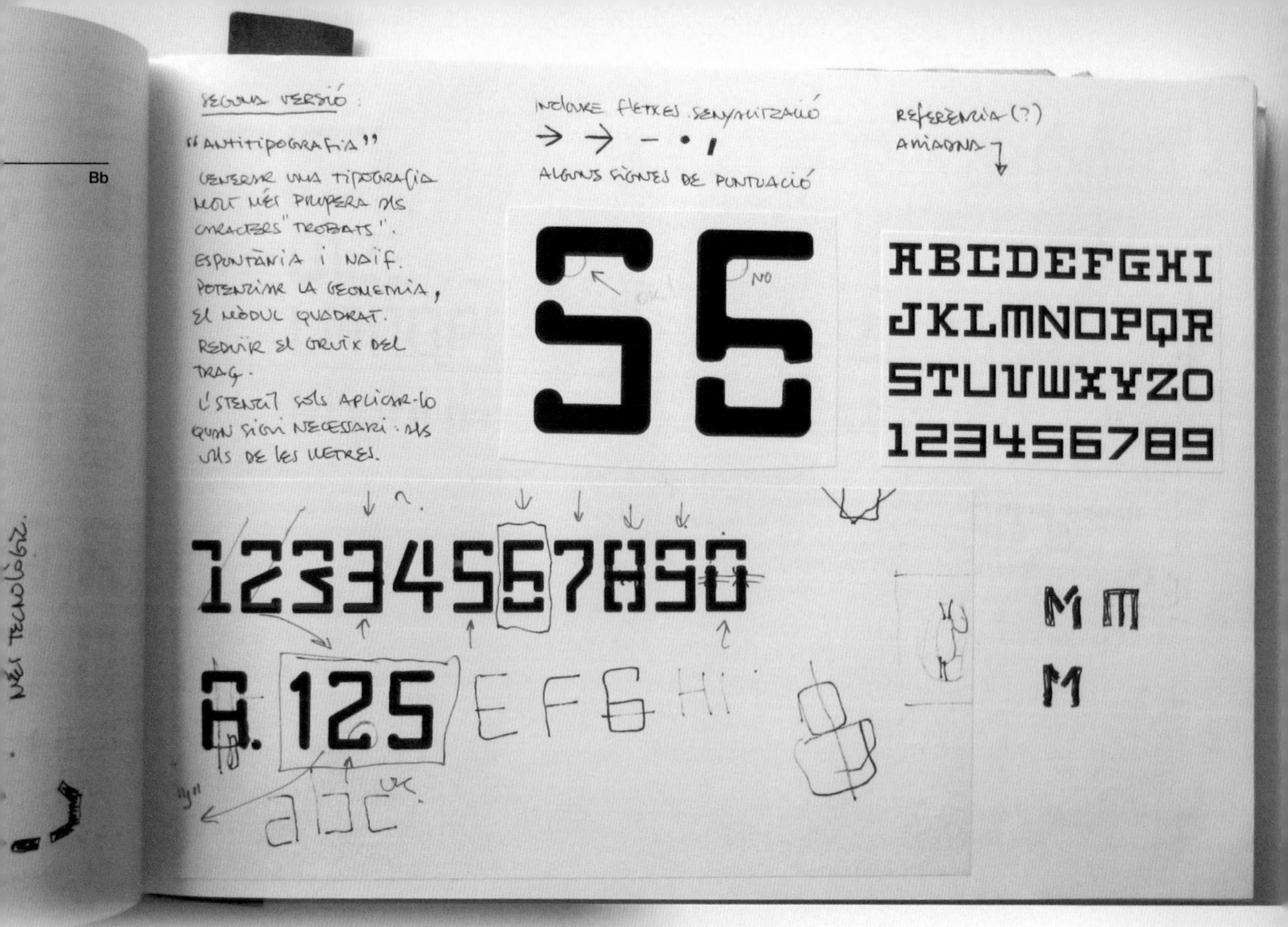

[handwritten notes, Catalan:]

SEGONA VERSIÓ:

"ANTITIPOGRAFIA"

GENERAR UNA TIPOGRAFIA MOLT MÉS PROPERA ALS CARACTERS "TROBATS".

ESPONTÀNIA i NAÏF.

POTENCIAR LA GEOMETRIA, EL MÒDUL QUADRAT.

REDUÏR EL GRUIX DEL TRAÇ.

L'STENCIL SOLS APLICAR-LO QUAN SIGUI NECESSARI · ALS UNS DE LES LLETRES.

INCLOURE FLETXES SENYALITZACIÓ

ALGUNS SIGNES DE PUNTUACIÓ

REFERÈNCIA (?)

AMIADONA

ABCDEFGHI
JKLMNOPQR
STUVWXYZ0
123456789

1233456789 0

A.125 EFGHI

abc

M M
M M

Andreu Balius

Barcelona-based designer Andreu Balius admits, "I've always had a notebook or sketchbook with me since I began working as a designer. When I think about a design project, a lecture, a type design, even when I travel, I carry a notebook where I take notes and record impressions of my travel experiences. In my sketchbooks you can find some printed ephemera glued on the pages, from currency notes to flyers or orange wrappers."

Balius considers his sketchbook to be a "route-book within my professional career." From his sketches he reviews his process: "It's like a long journey throughout my professional life, likes, expectations, wishes – together with drawings and chaotic notes. When I teach, I encourage my students to begin a sketchbook where the design process is recorded. This is a helpful way to understand our own process of work. It's our working experience becoming visible through paper spreads." However, he admits: "I do not consider myself a good illustrator. I just sketch things."

SUCCESS

Bb

through

PROJECTS

DIRECTION

George Bates

George Bates, an illustrator from Brooklyn, uses his sketchbooks to answer questions about process and aesthetics. "Each sketch has its place in the grander scheme of my work," he explains. "I've been quite surprised when sketches I've done as seemingly casual throwaway images become the actual final art for a project."

He is an inveterate hand-letterer and says, "I'm always surprised at how consistently excited people get about hand-lettered type. In high school I worked as an airbrush T-shirt artist at Great Adventure in New Jersey and it was surprising to me back then how people really got excited about this airbrushed/hand-lettered typography."

As for thematic consistency, he observes that "the books represent a place with no parameters, yet they also define what the parameters are. They emanate from a restless experimentation and curiosity with image-making, space, ideas, and plasticity. I do love that how a random or specific word or text that has been collaged, drawn, painted, or scratched into a page can manipulate and directly change the entire meaning of the image and that page as an experience. I do see the books as an ongoing, comprehensive, single work of art, but I haven't assigned a theme to them yet, as the understanding of them as a 'something' is continually evolving."

Charles and Ray Eames

ED ELLA

PAUL SCHER

SEYMOUR SEYMOUR
CHWAST CHWAST

Erwin K. Bauer

Viennese designer and design entrepreneur Erwin K. Bauer, who won the 2010 Joseph Binder Award for his typeface Reklame Stencil (opposite), looks at sketches as part of the design process and the project documentation. His typefaces include Sputnic Original Breitfett, Typopassage and Alpenmilchzentrale.

His goal as a sketcher is to visualize the initial typographic ideas and make the design vivid. "Most show steps in the design process," he says. "A lot takes place in the beginning, but the more you get to the final proposal the harder the struggle for the best detail becomes – it is the fight for the last 5 percent of quality. It is hard to reach, but it makes the difference. My sketchbook is more a loose collection of sketches, spread everywhere." Bauer openly admits that his sketches are full of "mistakes" and so provide "a document of many possible ways" of reaching a solution. "Sometimes it's a pity," he laments, "because you have to leave some good ideas behind, but they show up in other projects and contexts."

Das Bild des Thronfolgers Franz Ferdinand in der österrei-
chischen Öffentlichkeit war nicht von Beliebtheit geprägt.
Der Sohn des Bruders von Kaiser Franz Joseph, Karl Ludwig, war der nächste in der Erbfolge
auf den Thron Habsburgs, nachdem sein Cousin Rudolf 1889
in Mayerling Selbstmord begangen hatte.

ABCDEFGHIIJK
LMNOPQQQRST
UVWWXYZ YY
abcdefghijjklm-
nopqrstuvwxyz

abcdefghijklmn
opqrstuvwxyz
ABCDEFGHIJKLMNOP
QRSTUVWXYZ
1234567890 Jahr 1983
20. 05. 1875 18:47

wien
um
1930

café
elek-
trik

rotes
wien

peripherie
und
g'stättn

ins
freie

39

Donald Beekman

Housed on a ship on the river Amstel in Amsterdam, Donald Beekman is a designer with a penchant for keeping the remnants of his process. "I have two folders completely filled with sketches and sheets of paper with doodles and ideas dating back to 1990," he says. "I also have even earlier sketches, but those are kept in boxes with the printed items they were originally for." Not surprisingly, his sketch work serves as the starting point in all his designs. "I always sketch out an idea before getting in front of the screen. I can find pleasure in endless musing, but in general it has a goal."

And the goal is developing the perfect letter. "No matter where I am, I can always sit down and draw letters. It's a deficiency I learnt to take advantage of," he says. "These sketches contain the concepts of alphabets; you can really see the idea. This is how I develop my typefaces: it starts with a logo and almost immediately I try to see if I can draw the other characters that are not in the logo. This way I extend the idea to a working typeface. These very crude and simple sketches of a type treatment or a logo sometimes can lead to strong and beautiful typefaces. In my humble opinion, that is."

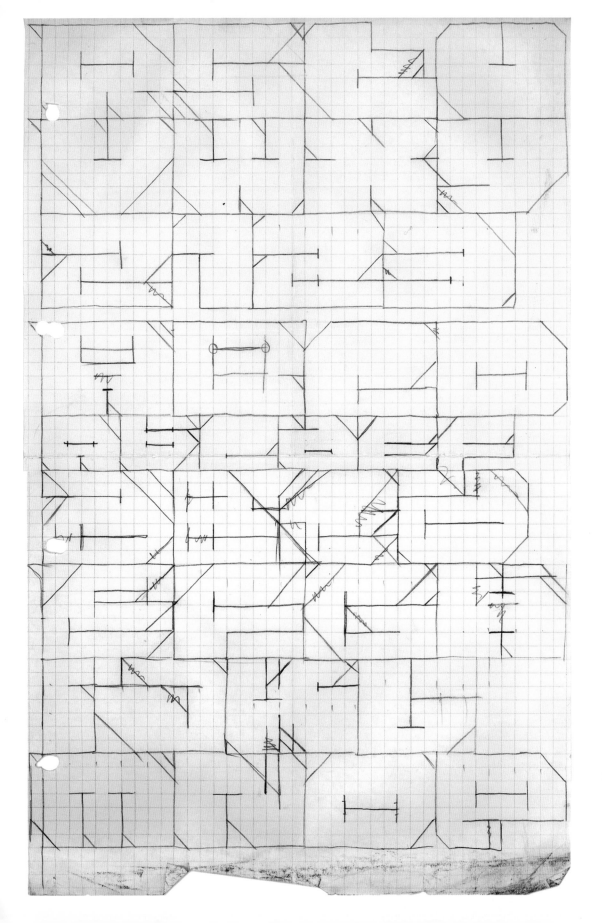

nnimu

ents a
she mi
own hous
low on
Lincoln
rnia tha
e makes
homely
a place
lucts
clients
ow she
ouse
gals
trial

assymetric serifs

Bb

nimhua
imntjk
v w w m

no contrast

completely
without
serifs

k
k

n ①
n ②
n ③

m ① m ②

a g   ascender

nearly
monolinear

f + j + r

f r J C

growin
evusf

n

Ligan

Greta
9 Octo
Typ

slanted?

smaller?

الكـربية

| w: 592 | w: 408 | w: 321 | w: 571 | w: 724 | w: 342 | w: 261 |
| | | | l: -66 | r: 0 | l: 0 | r: 0 | |

الخططوط

| l: -5 | w: 737 | r: 40 | l: 50 | w: 529 | r: 0 | l: 0 | w: 817 | r: 0 | w: 700 | w: 342 | w: 261 |

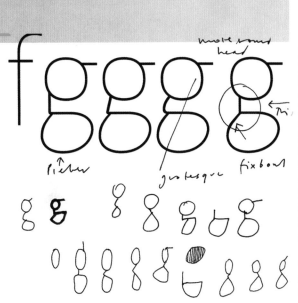

Peter Bilak

Peter Bilak's studio in The Hague, Netherlands, specializes in the creation of custom fonts. He has designed several fonts for FontShop International, founded Typotheque foundry, co-founded *Dot Dot Dot* magazine and gives talks and workshops around the world. He has been sketching ever since he was young, he explains, but adds, "In the arts, there is a tendency today to consider sketches (e.g. Old Masters' drawings) on their own, and to sell them as autonomous artworks. This has to do with creating added value, and is far from the artist's original intention. While I am presenting a selection of sketches here, omitting those that didn't help the creating process, it is important not to consider them on their own, but as a tool to generate possibilities."

Bilak says there is not always a clear purpose to sketches: "Sometimes I draw just for the joy of drawing. My sketches are usually tiny and very rough – they are meant as the first translation of an abstract idea into visual form. If I see that there is a potential for a new typeface, I don't make more elaborate sketches but start working digitally," he says.

43

Nobody can read
this type.

You ~~want~~
boring, I'll give you
~~boring.~~

Boring is beside
the point.
Legibility...

..is
~~white~~
bread.

Please don't interrupt.
Look, language is meant
to communicate.

RIGHT ON.

And type has to
COMMUNICATE
WHAT'S (AROUND) US.

What's around us
is MEANING.

And that
~~meaning is~~
DISORDER.

ART is
never
disorder.

Maybe your art isn't.
It's all neat and
packaged.

Art may be
▷ NEAT but it is
never
~~packaged!!~~

Now
you're
Talking!

R. O. Blechman

For over fifty-five years, according to his own calculation, R. O. Blechman, veteran New York illustrator, comics artist, animator, and author, with short and feature-length animated films to his name, has kept a notebook to jot down ideas as they occur to him. "I always keep writing material by my bedside, and rarely travel without having paper and pen handy. I never know when an idea will strike. When my ideas take verbal form I put down a word or a sentence or even a few paragraphs."

For Blechman, being prolific is simply hardwired into his brain and his sketchbooks are an extension of this. They continue to serve as reference for present and possible future projects. They are also a respite from the more formal work he does. "My sketches can be awful (sloppy) or great (fresh)," he says. "I never know what will turn up in my jottings." These comic sketches from 1997 are not typical of the typographic sketches found in the rest of this book, but indicate the importance Blechman places on type design and communication.

Matteo Bologna

A native of Italy, Matteo Bologna is the founder and principal of Mucca Design in New York. His multidisciplinary background in architecture, graphic design, illustration, and typography triggered his decision to create a New York branding and design agency that emphasizes typography as a signature conceit.

Sketching is a reluctant part of his routine, used "to quickly freeze something that I've already designed in my mind." Usually they do not last more than few weeks. Once they are done they end up in the 'circular file.' I'm for the preservation of bytes, not atoms."

With that in mind, he says, he usually hates sketching on paper. "So the real function is a reminder of some passing thoughts. They are imprecise and do not contain all the info that I know I'll add once transformed in a digital file."

When asked what the single most unusual aspect of his images is, Bologna responds: "They suck." So much for the art of imperfection.

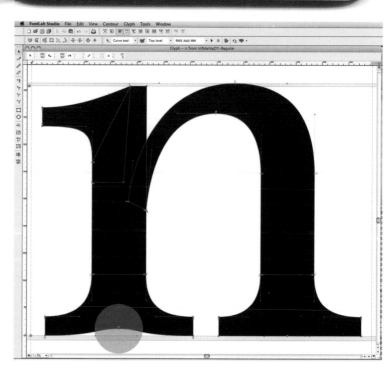

SHAWN COLVIN / EARL & RANDY SCRUGGS / ROSANNE CASH
WILLIE NELSON / THE WHITES / RICKY SKAGGS / JUNE CARTER
CASH / THE NITTY GRITTY DIRT BAND / GEORGE JONES
SHERYL CROW / EMMYLOU HARRIS / PEASALL SISTERS / THE DEL
McCOURY BAND / JOHNNY CASH / MARTY STUART / JANET & JOE CARTER

The
UNbROKEN
CiRCLe

SWALLOW The SeA

MATTHEW
PERRYMAN
JONES

THE
UNBROKEN CIRCLE

Wayne,
    Just got back in town yesterday. I am totally thrilled with the finished product. Your work is beautiful. Look forward to working with you more in the future,
    JCC
                                                    6-3-04

Circle

THE
UN
BROKEN
CIRCLE

THE
UNBROKEN
CIRCLE

UNBROKE

THE
UNBROKEN
CIRCLE

THE MUSICAL HERITAGE OF THE
CARTER FAMILY

THE
UNBROKEN
CIRCLE

Wayne Brezinka

Minneapolis-born Wayne Brezinka's Brezinka Design Co. specializes in illustration, hand-lettering, and design. He has maintained a sketchbook for twelve years – "as long as I've been freelancing and working for myself," he says. "I have specific projects and assignments going on that require clear thinking prior to executing the final. I like to get my thoughts out whenever the urge arises." Still, he notes, his sketchbooks are "uninhibited chaos."

"More often than not," he adds, "my sketches are thoughts and ideas being worked into an existing assignment. I like to consider composition and layout and how the type may or may not work within it."

Brezinka's drawings are pretty raw and "some of the letters, shapes, and forms are not as refined as I'd like them to be, so I usually tweak them prior to completion of the finished work," he explains. "Sometimes the sketch ends up being used as the final rendering. I've slowly learned that the first subconscious thought and doodle is more often than not the best and strongest idea."

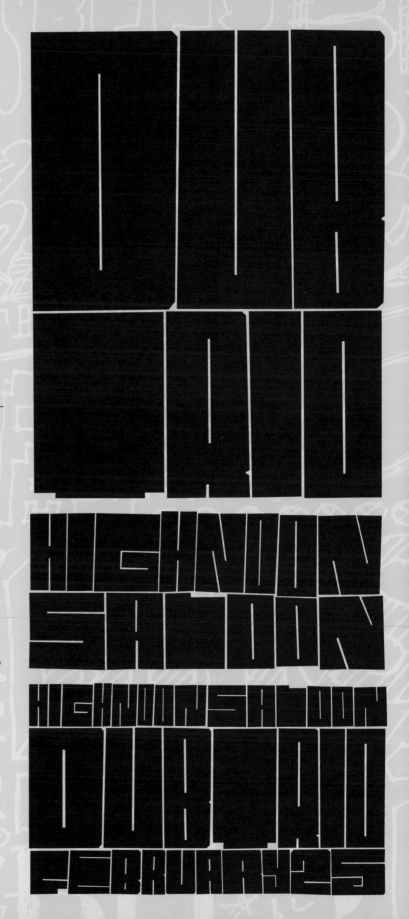

Travis Cain

Travis Cain, a designer and art director based in New York, is the designer of a gaggle of Kidrobot vinyl toys, including Dunny Series 2009 Wood Chases, Cheeze and Ribeye Dunnys, and Kidrobot BFFs. Making letterforms, however, is among his favorite pastimes. "Generally, my sketches are type experiments, playing with forms, hand-lettered type, and type as pattern," he says. Cain's sketches usually find their way into his work – "Maybe not directly, but I might find a use for letterforms I sketched in a poster, illustration, or other personal project."

These sketches are more experimental and loose than he can normally be in his daily work. "I work for a cosmetics company whose style is much more classic – which I enjoy as well – but it is great to let go and not worry so much about whether or not someone can read what I am making."

Most of his sketches involve making type. "Designing letters that can be a bit of a challenge for the viewer to read intrigues me. I intentionally take elements that make a letterform recognizable and exaggerate them, so that a short sentence becomes a bold pattern. I also like strange phrases like 'see what I'm saying' and visualizing poor communication – we often talk to one another, but don't really say anything."

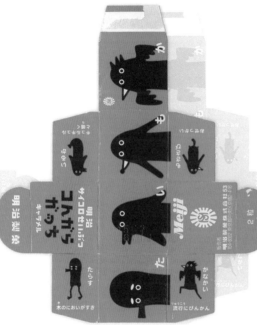
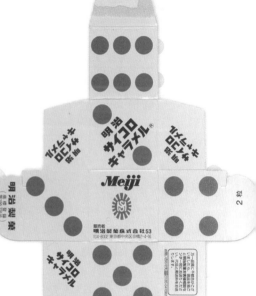

Brian Cairns

Glasgow-based illustrator and designer Brian Cairns has been a
devoted sketchbooker for over twenty years. "They are visual notes
to myself," he declares. "I am often rushing somewhere when I come
across something that interests me and it is simply quicker to take
a photograph. If it is something that is more conceptual and not so
easily documented photographically then I will do a quick sketch that
only really makes sense to myself." It is a form of visual shorthand
to jog his memory. "I tend to process the images later and distill the
aspect that interested me. The link between the sketch and finished
works is not always obvious, and the translation of the idea is part of
the process."

The sketches are unique as "the evidence of a human hand in
the process, either in the imperfections, or in the consideration given
to a placement of elements that is perfectly appropriate in a not-so-
obvious way." His thematic preference in these sketches from 2000
to 2009 is best described as "type as image" – "often I am looking at
the aesthetic of the type rather than the message or context."

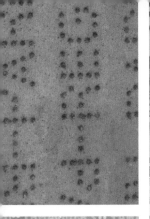

Pequeños
MUSICAL
LAS ESTRELLAS
☆ ANDINAS
SABADO
24
JULIO-99
CHIRINOS
Club
SEPULTUREROS
Un Lugar Diferente
NAPOLITANO
En Piano
Show Bar Diferente
POKAR DE REYNAS
Los Incontenibles
Gatos
Negros
California
Dancing Club
EL PALACIO DEL BAILE EN MEXICO
DESCARGA

GRUPO
CHAMAI
GRUPO
Libertad
Sonido
Ilusion
Sconstelacion
VIERNES
6
AGOSTO 1999
SUPERGRUPO
COLOMBIA
SABADO 7 AGOSTO 1999
LA UNICA SONORA
MARACAIBO
grupo
Yassy's
GRUPO LA
TIR...

Pigarenm
BER

まごっち缶バッジ2
全15種
BANDAI
S•• TAMAGOTCH'S •• TAM

INRIT VRY HOUDEN
Hout transport.
Dank u

149

JACKSON
CHORLEY

HALIFAX
TO THE
FRONT

6 2
4 A

LUCHA
AR
XOCHI
XOCHIMILCO CENTRO A
DOMINGO 2
FUNCION DE CA
VILLANO 3 REVANCHA EN
SUPER LIBRE
VS

CABELLERA V
TONY GIRIO
CHOQUE DE
JAQUE MATI
Y REY VIKINGO »
DOC MARKUZ DOC LA
Y DOC SPIQUIAT
Black MAN Jr HOMBRE ARANA Y BLACK S
HIPNOSIS AVERNOSIS BESTIA MACM

Bold   13
Bold   19¼
Black   24½
Ultra   29¾

Bold   12
Black   16½
Ultra   21
   25½

Matthew Carter

Matthew Carter, born in London and based in Cambridge, Massachusetts, is one of the pioneers of digital type design. His career, however, began in the hot metal shops, starting aged nineteen as Jan van Krimpen's assistant in the Netherlands. Carter has designed typefaces for Linotype, including Bell Centennial. With Mike Parker he founded Bitstream, one of the first digital foundries, before forming Carter and Cone in 1991 with Cherie Cone. His most frequently used digital font is Verdana.

His types have been widely used for their aesthetic and functional virtues. Although much of the finishing work is done on computer,

Carter has never lost the pleasure of working on paper. Included here are: a diagram of the four weights of Galliard Roman and Italic (ink on Cronaflex, 1978); early sketches for Bitstream Charter Roman and Italic (pencil on tracing paper, 1986); an experiment in the use of "half-bitting" to smooth curves (ink on Cronaflex, 1980); and, overleaf, trial sketches for Bell Centennial, Carter's typeface for use in American telephone directories (ink on Cronaflex, 1976). "The plan was to derive the new directory typeface from Helvetica," he explains. "Trial characters such as these, reduced photographically to actual size, proved hard to read; the eventual design took a different direction."

hopivna

hopiva

hopiva

mtdeu

vivgsly

mtedcr

mtedcr

natesa

irycbz

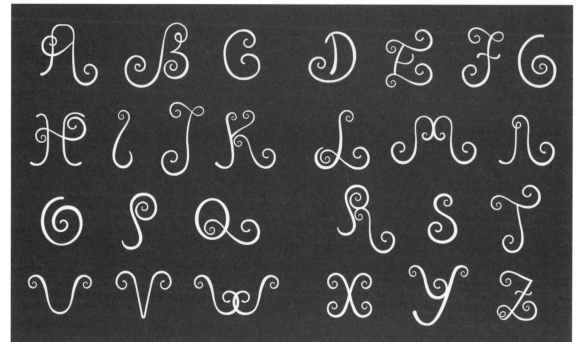

Celina Carvalho

Brazilian designer Celina Carvalho has kept sketchbooks since the beginning of college. "There are two main purposes for doing sketches," she says. "The first one is when I want to register what I see, when the images are very fresh in my mind. The second is to get started on the project. When I haven't had ideas yet, sometimes I find it harder to begin designing directly on the computer. With the sketchbook I can simply scribble with no concerns. I draw whatever comes to mind, even if it has nothing to do with what I

need to achieve. And this leads me to the beginning of my ideas." The images here show Carvalho's drawings of iron motifs found in the gates, balconies, and windows of Venice. "They inspired me to create letters, which would be the starting point for me to develop unique alphabets." She likes the way one subject or image becomes something else, and in the sketches here, she enjoys "how something can emerge with a completely different purpose (for example, a window iron motif turns into a letter C, which turns into a pattern)."

ABCDEF
GHIJKL
MNOPQR
STUVWX
YZabca
befghijk
lmnopq
rstuvw
xyzimi

Rodrigo Xavier Cavazos

Rodrigo Xavier Cavazos (RXC) is principal of PSY/OPS Type Foundry in San Francisco and instructor in typeface design at California College of the Arts.

Cavazos remarks that "the softer, wobblier edges of the sketch make it possible to envision nuanced variations in a way that's different from vector forms. When sketching I try not to retrace anything I've drawn before, even where the same motif is expected to repeat. This yields multiple variants of curves and shapes, and I can then choose the best ones when I start to draft the clean forms. The slight variations in form definitely enliven sketch art in a way that is typically lost in the final art, where letters are built in a more mechanical, cookie-cutter manner."

"In past years, sketches have mainly been casual explorations for my own ideas," he explains. "Lately, with less open time, sketching is mainly reserved for client projects. Some of the sketches have been scanned and refined in Photoshop, then printed back out and redrawn in order to infuse nuance or character, or just make changes quickly and intuitively." Most of these images have, he notes, been "tucked away for ten or twelve years, and others range up through last year. I'd forgotten about a lot of the older, more whimsical art."

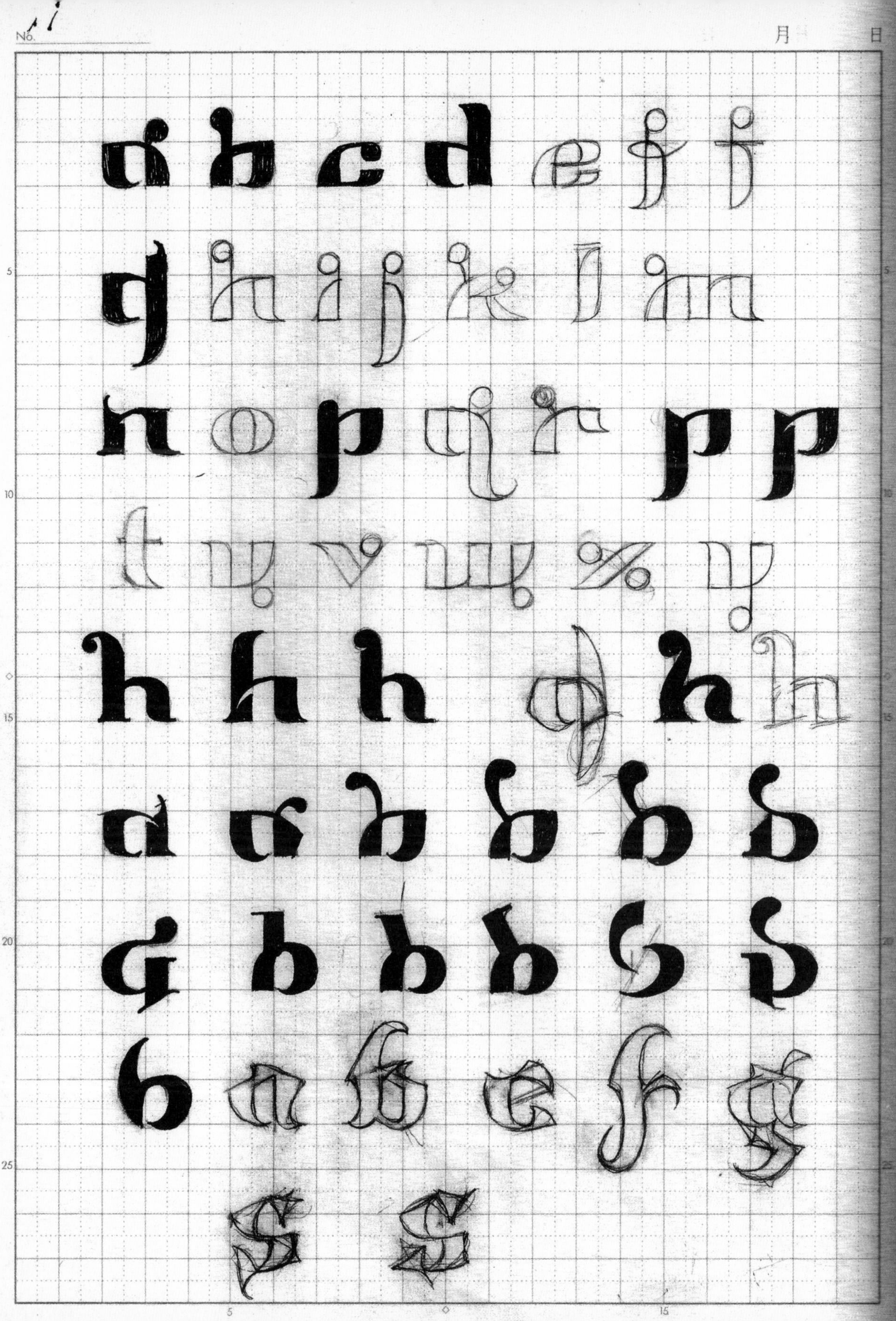
No. 11
月
日

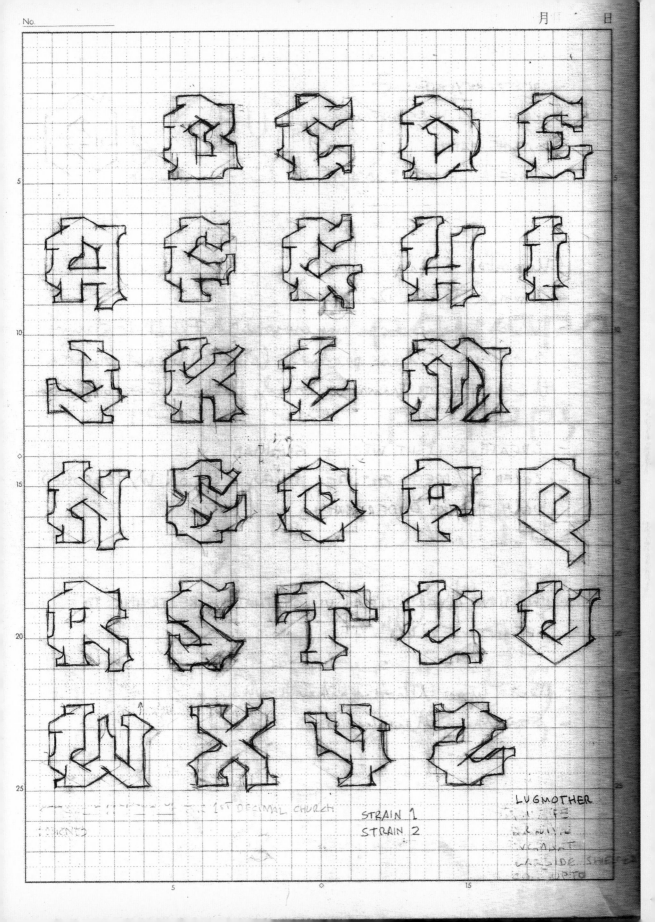

1ST DECIMAL CHURCH

STRAIN 1
STRAIN 2

LUGMOTHER

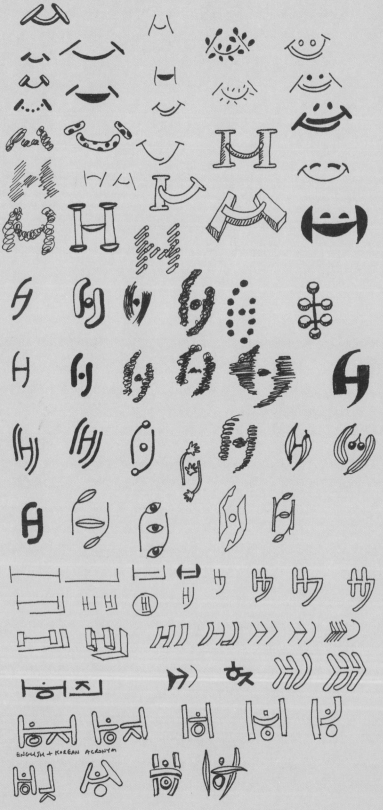

HOW TO EXPRESS H & HAPPINESS = SMILE

ENGLISH + KOREAN ACRONYM

Don Ryun Chang

Don Ryun Chang, a designer and educator from Seoul, South Korea, who was educated in New York, has sketchbooks that date back several decades. "They are a manifestation of ideas and purely initial explorations and studies. I end up circling possible directions with a red marker and putting them up on the wall to digest and later refine."

Chang is often transfixed by his sketch work. "They have the human element, which is expressed in crooked, non-uniform lines," he explains. "It allows me to see the full range of expressions from mundane and silly to radical and innovative. In this sense, they have a life of their own."

All these exploratory sketches from February 2010 belong to a project on which he is advising for a brand consulting company. They are works in progress prior to finalizing in Illustrator. "The common theme is how to express different concepts for Hite Jinro, which is a Korean distiller company that is famous for beers and Korean *soju*, but is planning to branch out into different food and beverage industries," he explains. "The new brand theme is the 'culture of positivity' and thus in some forms there is an intent to show happiness and other pleasant icons."

HOW TO EXPRESS + H J

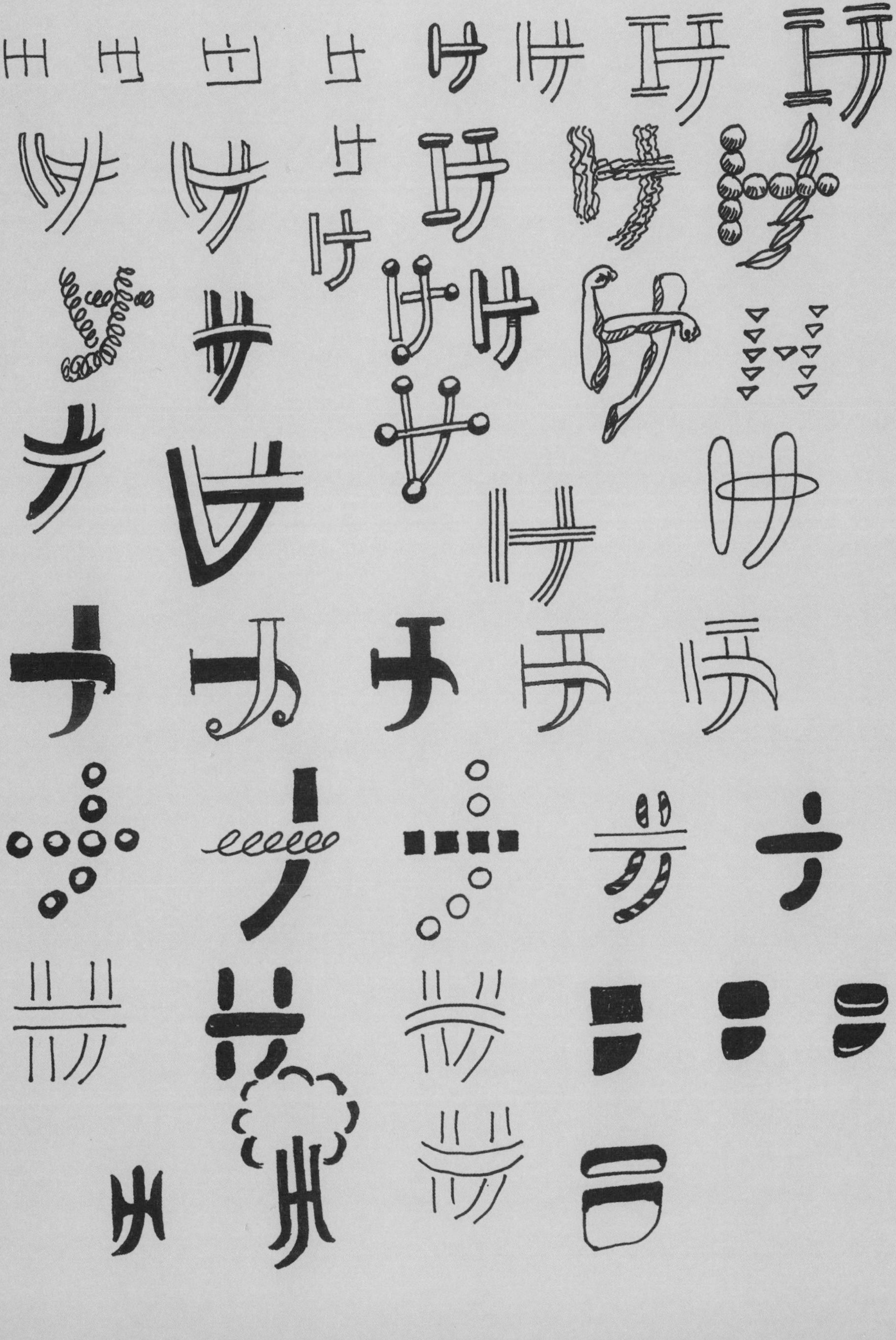

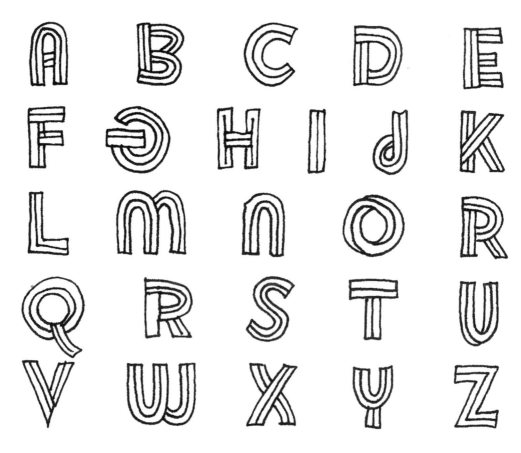

Chank Diesel

Canadian-born, Florida-raised type designer Chank Diesel (aka Charles Andermack) designs display typefaces and creates custom fonts for corporations, including Taco Bell, Tanqueray, and Ocean Spray. He says that sketching has an educative effect – it is what he calls "alphabet practice:" "Seems like you can be great at anything if you practice a lot, so I practice drawing the alphabet," he says. What's more, "an artist often gets an idea stuck in his head, and can spend all their time going round and round thinking about it. So I do a sketch just to get the idea out of my head. And once it's on paper, you get a new vantage point, and can more easily see which direction your idea should go, or if it should be abandoned. I can do a sketch in a few minutes, but I'll spend hours refining it and adding extra language support and spacing and kerning. But I always try to keep a human element somewhere in the final fonts. It's all the funny little flaws and bugs in my work that set it apart from others'."

Every drawing gets a number – he started this circa 1994. "My original intent was to break Picasso's productivity record by making over a million works of art. Now I'm not quite that ambitious, but I still number everything. I've made over 16,000 of these over the years."

#9845: ROBERT DOWNEY Jr.

GOOD LUCK!

BORN
APRIL 4, 1965

WON A GOLDEN GLOBE
FOR HIS ROLE on ALLY McBEAL
WANDERED INTO HIS NEIGHBOR'S HOUSE,
SNL CAST MEMBER 85-86
SON'S NAME IS INDIO
ANTHONY MICHAEL HALL IS INDIO'S GODFATHER • STARRED IN ELTON JOHN VIDEO "I WANT LOVE"

www.mugshots.net

INVOLVED
WITH SARAH
JESSICA PARKER
FOR 7 YEARS.
JAILED FOR DRUG CHARGES.
URINE TESTED POSITIVE FOR
MORPHINE, HEROIN, MARIJUANA
VALIUM & COCAINE
BRITISH ACADEMY AWARD FOR CHAPLIN

SERVED PRISON TIME FOR HIS DRUG USE and WAS ARRESTED at MERV GRIFFIN'S RESORT-O-TEL.

M. Chank 7-31-01

www.CHANK.com
BOX 580736
MINNEAPOLIS, M
55458-0736

67

A ΛBCΔΣ

#16,005
12.31.2009

#16050 WWW.CHANK.COM
2/21/2010
M. Chahtopn

www.clockwork.net
clock work

Art Chantry

Art Chantry, pioneer of Seattle punk music and theater posters, does not always keep sketchbooks, although he uses his hands more than the computer. These pages show sketches, comps, and progressives for PROSPERO, a project promoted by an old friend and co-worker who was starting up as an Internet distribution-promotion-mentor for documentary films.

The name comes from Shakespeare's *The Tempest*: the character Prospero is, among other things, a trickster and magician. The mark was based on ideas of theater, American industrial iconography, and magic. "The process boiled along at a slow pace," Chantry explains, "constantly coming up with new ideas while refining and fine-tuning earlier ideas." Ultimately three of the designs were chosen: one as a corporate and general identity, one for a bug and eventual use as a mark for a children's film site, and one for use on industrial documentary work." Apparently, the client couldn't quite make up his mind.

The process took nine months but the client was unable to find financing. "This was all during 2008 and the economy tanked just as they were seeking investment," says Chantry. "They still have a small Internet presence and the primary logo seems to be in use, but bastardized into a weak outline form."

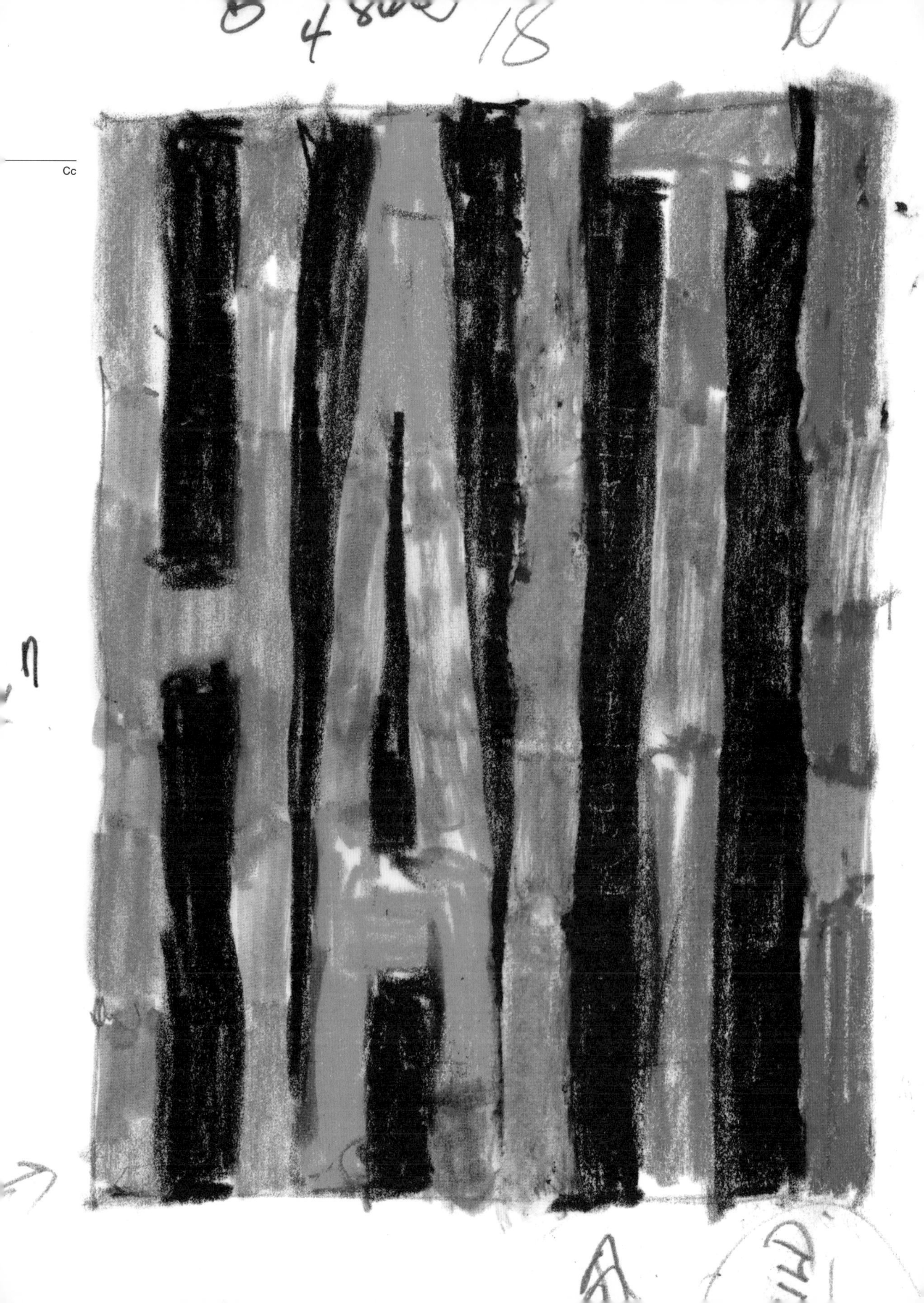

Ivan Chermayeff

American Modernist Ivan Chermayeff is a founding partner of Chermayeff & Geismar in New York (see also page 126), and has created much memorable corporate identity, brand development, and logo design. Chermayeff's trademarks, posters, publications, and art installations for contemporary buildings are widely recognized and many of his oldest works are still in currency.

Having worked long before the advent of the computer, Chermayeff still does most of his initial concept work with pencil and paper, and yet, "I hardly ever keep sketches. What you have is because they're current," he says about his raw scribbles, but they do serve an important purpose. "I usually have to plan ahead a little, especially if it's design rather than illustration, and I often give them to staff to execute on computer."

Included here are a rough sketch for a poster supporting Doctors Without Borders (the torn letters of Haiti), and rough personal sketches for an experiment in mixing up what is seen or said in the mind with what can actually be done in paint or paper, ignoring the conventional use and break-up of words. Chermayeff called this "Dysfunctionalandoutofsyncexperiments-inreadingandseeing."

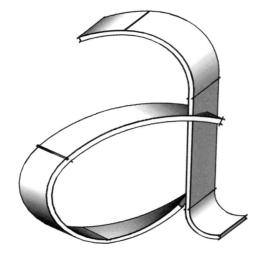

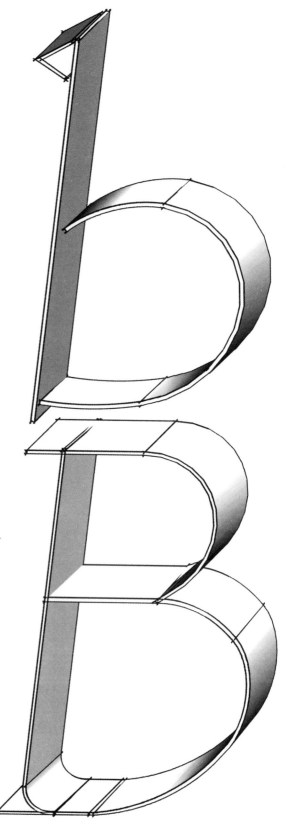

Todd Childers

Todd Childers is a graphic designer and Associate Professor of
Graphic Design at the School of Art at Bowling Green State University
in Ohio. "I've been sketching letters since 1977, long before I knew
what graphic design or type design was," he says. Eventually he
sketched letters as a prelude to designing logotypes and this evolved
into typeface design. Childers was inspired by the typographic
studies in Ed Fella's sketchbooks, Jeffery Keedy's font designs, and
font designers Phil Baines and Jonathan Barnbrook.

Mostly, Childers's sketches are "pure exploration and testing
ideas." Very few of his sketches get applied to developing a new
font. "I try to find ways to combine the unexpected," he says about
his sketch work. "I am interested in synthesizing fonts from the
combination of geometric sans serif with traditional black-letter or
modern with Medieval versals. This idea is probably derived from my
graduate studies at CalArts [California Institute of the Arts], where
we studied the principles of deconstruction. I am at ease looking
forwards and backwards at the same time. In other words, I try to be
aware of history and open to the future."

H A
U K
G W

Shape
of my Heart

Shape
of my Heart

Shape
of my Heart

La magia del fare.
The charm of making.

La magia del fare
The charm of making

La magia del fare.

La magia del fare.
The charm of making.

The charm of making.

La magia del fare.
The charm of making.

La magia del fare.
The charm of making.

La magia del fare

James Clough

James Clough, a Milan-based English designer, typographer, calligrapher, and inscriptions scholar, has "hung on to his sketches" (pieces of calligraphy and lettering) since becoming a freelancer about thirty years ago. They give him a certain amount of solace. "I keep them and make selections that I show to clients," he reports. "Usually, for a logo, a label or whatnot, I make dozens of variously written ideas. I also keep them for personal reference. They occasionally supply inspiration for new jobs."

The sketches are "a serious game," he adds. "Often I feel that it is the pen, pencil, or brush that controls my hand. Each instrument has its own preferences of style. More often than not, in recent years clients have become fussier and require tons of different ideas. Up to a point I learn from the client, but coming up with many different solutions is also the client's way of sorting out his own mind and getting his ideas straight." Variety is the key word in Clough's lexicon, "and that is also a necessity for any calligrapher who offers his or her services to today's publishers, advertisers, or businessmen. The written word has infinite possibilities of shape. The professional calligrapher can evoke ambience, feelings, and much more by use of different tools, writing with them at varying speeds in many styles."

Elaine Lustig Cohen

Elaine Lustig Cohen began designing in the early 1950s while working for her husband, Alvin Lustig. Blinded by diabetes, he would dictate his type and color preferences to his wife and other assistants. Cohen learned much about typefaces from this process. After Lustig died in 1955, Cohen assumed the studio's work and clients, producing scores of book covers and jackets and works in various other media.

The studio closed in 1967, and although Cohen continued to design catalog covers for Ex Libris, the antiquarian bookstore she and author Arthur Cohen ran together, focusing on avant-garde Modernist books and documents, she turned instead to making art inspired, in part, by Constructivism, Dada, and the Bauhaus. To celebrate her eightieth birthday in 2007, she produced a series of five *giclée* (high-quality inkjet) prints in a limited edition of five each, which pay homage to her life in graphic design.

The series came about "as I became involved in creating alphabets in Adobe Illustrator," she says, "which led to exploring all kinds of measurements." The first one, which is not included in the edition, was a regular yellow folding ruler where she substituted the numbers 1–26 with the 26 letters of the alphabet, called "Letter Meter." "My eye then naturally fell on other devices on my desk which use measurements," she says, and the unnamed series evolved to include a decorative alphabet and a chessboard.

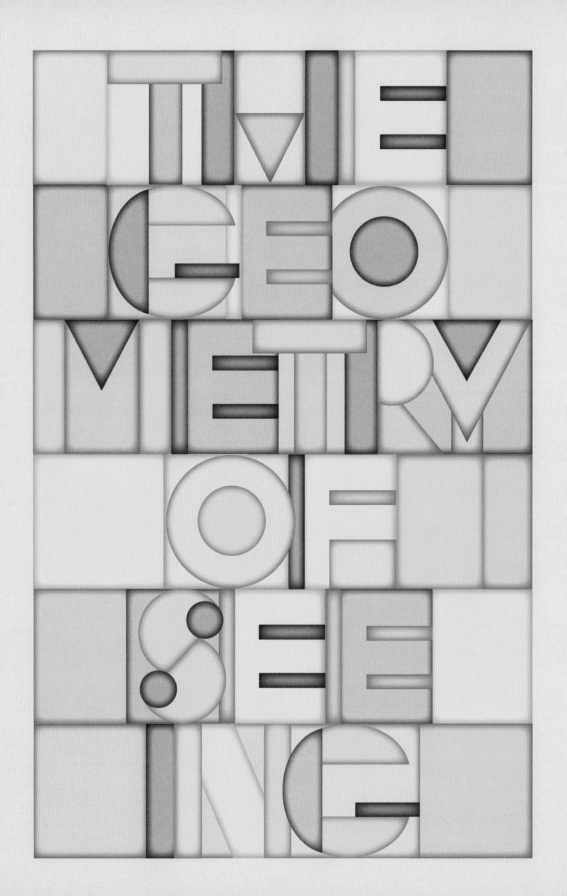

THE GEOMETRY OF SEEING

Kevin Cornell

Kevin Cornell, an illustrator and designer based in Philadelphia and founder of the website Bearskinrug, uses a sketchbook to figure out "how I want to handle a specific word or phrase – usually the title of a comic, or a logo or something. But pretty often I just get a hankering to play around, and I'll write out gibberish just so I can explore the letterforms."

He notes that "what I think is attractive about sketchbooks (and sketches in general) is that most of the time they communicate almost everything you'd look to communicate in the final piece." He further offers the theory that "most illustrators use sketchbooks to help figure out visual problems, and so, on the same spread, or across spreads, you might find the same thing drawn from different perspectives, or perhaps a couple of options for how to treat a piece of text. They're just filled with lovely little vignettes. I rarely use sketchbooks that way. In a sense, these are more akin to a diary than a sketchbook. Just a guy unloading the crap from his head." The book shown here is from spring 2005.

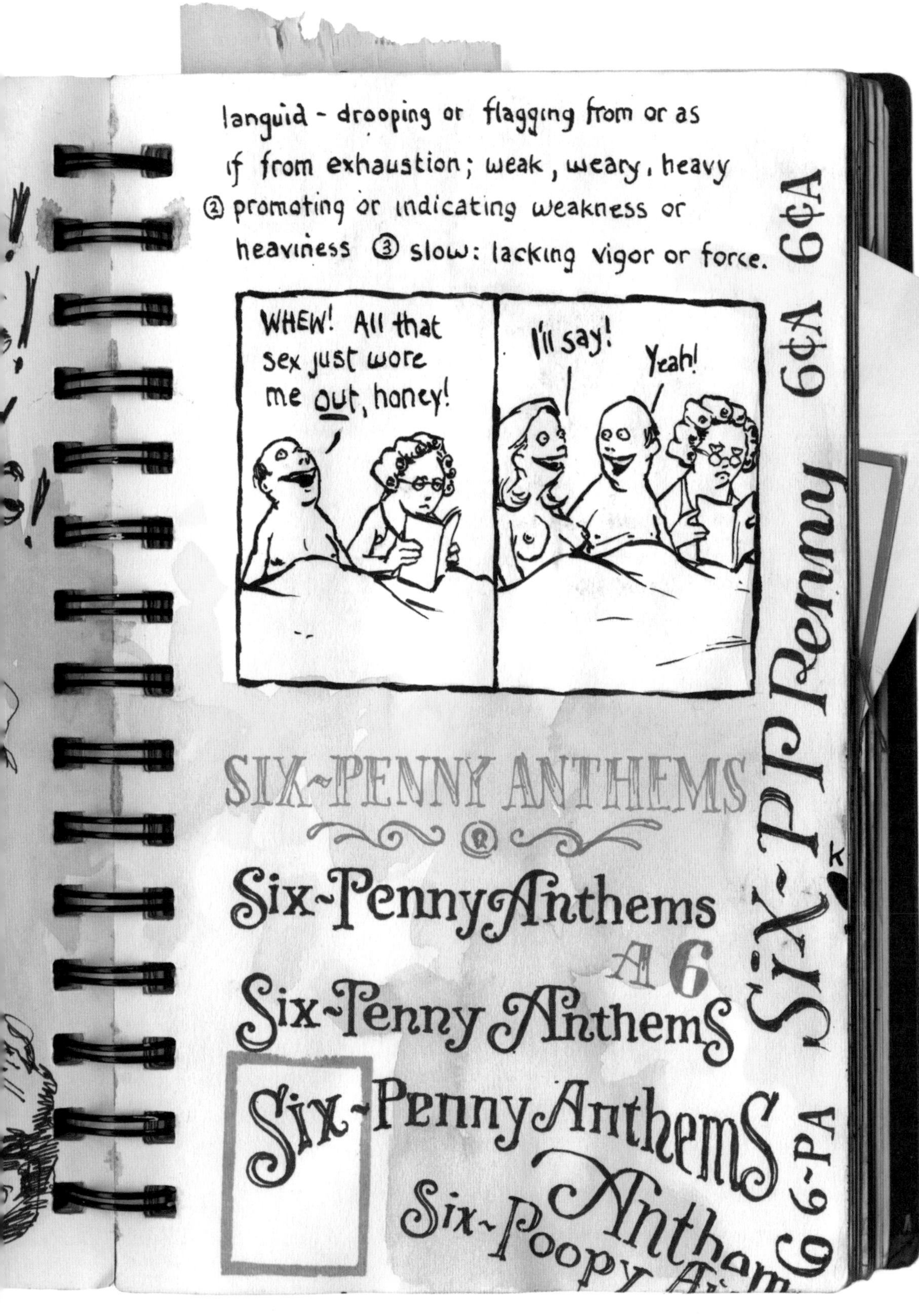

languid - drooping or flagging from or as
if from exhaustion; weak, weary, heavy
② promoting or indicating weakness or
heaviness ③ slow: lacking vigor or force.

SIX~PENNY ANTHEMS

Six~Penny Anthems
A 6
Six~Penny Anthems
Six~Penny Anthems
Six~Poopy A...

DESIC
S
CON
CHINESE
DRAGON
De
DESSICAMEL

SUCKS THE MOISTURE
FROM HIS ENEMIES

GOTTA KEEP CLEAN!
GOTTA get RID of the GERMS!
YOU'D BE WISE TO DO THE SAME!
eh! EH!

Margaret Cusack

Brooklyn-based Margaret Cusack creates stitched illustration, embroidered samplers, quilted artwork, soft sculpture, props, stock images, and portraits – all done with needle and thread.

"I've always created sketches, though I usually don't use a sketchbook," she says about the laborious process. "Because I am an illustrator and my husband is an art director and our daughter is a jewelry/costume designer, there is always a supply of 'scrap paper' at every table in our house, so that we can quickly get our ideas across to the others with a quick sketch using pencil and paper." Her sketches are used "to begin the process. When I get an assignment

I write down a few words for each of my thumbnail ideas that I sketch on paper – sometimes as postage stamp-sized sketches. Then I do a larger sketch (about 5" × 4" or smaller) of the ones that I decide to pursue. I rough out up to ten or more concepts. Many are created quickly and others are based on reference images that I keep in my files. (I have several folders of typography references – with at least one titled 'Favorites.') Each of my sketches has the 'germ' of a different idea." Unlike Cusack's final stitching, the sketches have fluidity and rawness. "It's great to not deal with the details and angst that comes with completing the finished artwork," she says.

To America With Love

It's All A Big Nothing

A Special Visit

October 14, 1997 • Vol. XLII No. 41 • America['s Large]st Weekly Newspaper • www.villagevoice.com

the village VOICE

FREE

Whip Me, Honey!

S/M Goes Mainstream

BY GUY TREBAY

Radoje Dedić

Serbian-born graphic designer and typographer Radoje Dedić, currently living in Los Angeles, is an inveterate "conceptual designer," working with signs, symbols, metaphor, and allegory – like so many of his country's designers.

Type is a significant part of his output, and he has drawn letters in sketchbooks, he says, since he was little. "Actually, my mum keeps it all in one old broken fridge in our apartment in Serbia," he says. The sketches shown here, from 2009 to 2010, are drawings that Dedić did in the United States. They are used to "work out my ideas, whether personal or commercial," and find the way into various other things." But they are "very hard for me to keep because I'm moving a lot from place to place."

"The sketches I make almost always define the shape of my final projects," he notes. "My end results are sometimes aesthetically different than what I planned in my sketchbook, but the underlying concept had usually been worked out beforehand."

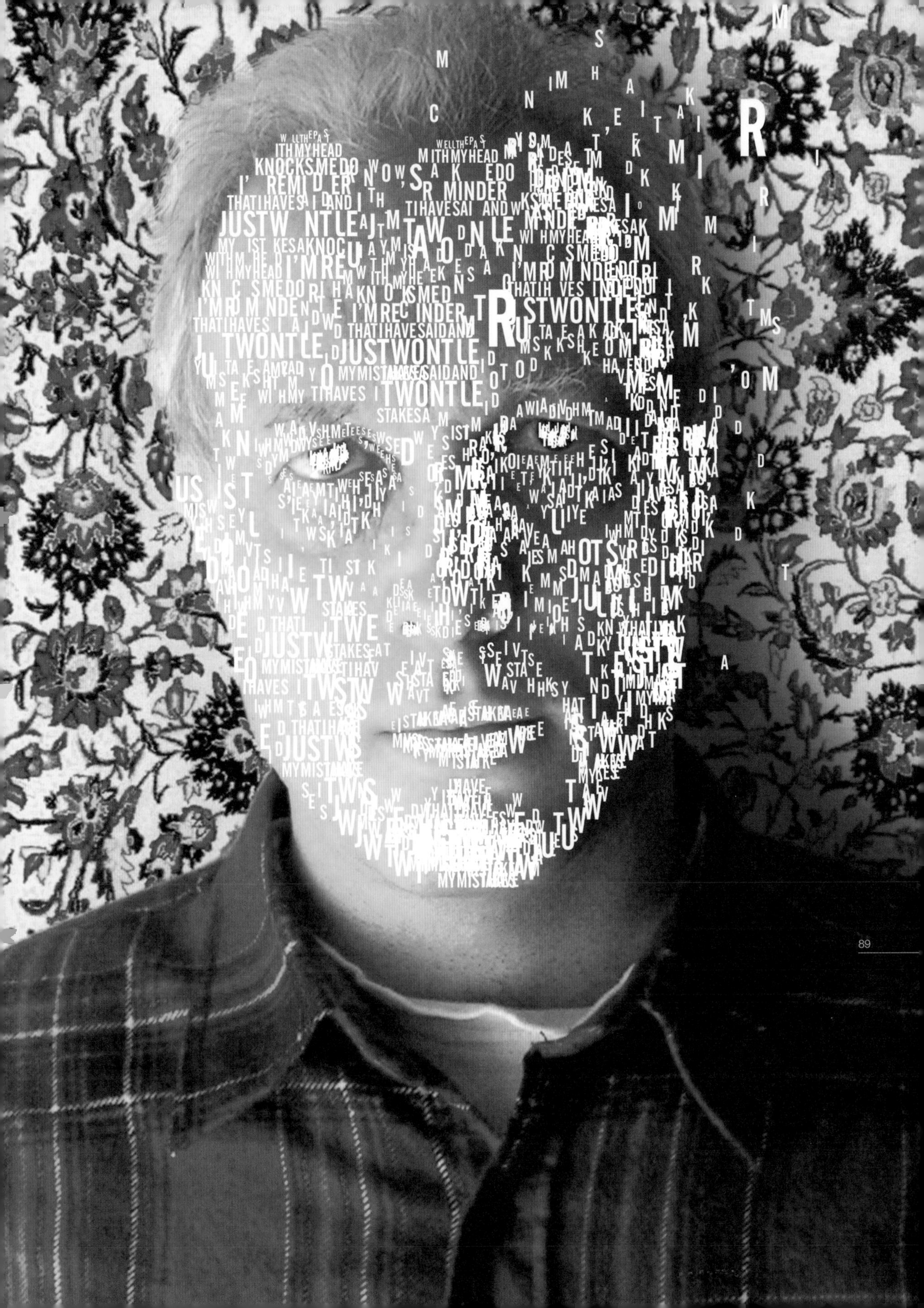
ITHMYHEAD
KNOCKSMEDO
JUSTWONTLE
MYMISTAKE

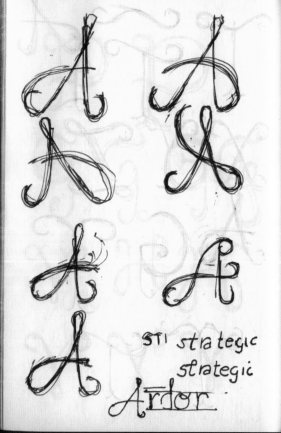

STI strategic
strategic
Ardor

Roberto de Vicq de Cumptich

Roberto de Vicq de Cumptich, whose New York studio specializes in book covers, and who has authored children's books devoted to type, has kept sketchbooks, he says, "since forever. My sophomore project teacher forced us all to carry one. All ideas had to be sketched out and presented with the final project. Thank God for the 'European shoulder bag' for men, made it much easier to carry it. Also thank God for Jack Spade, who designed one that does not make you look like a dork."

He uses his mighty books "to keep a record of all the ideas flying around in my head and to try different quick variations of each one, without being bogged down by finalizing it. I normally sketch when there are too many variables, and it is a way of organizing, prioritizing, and editing my ideas. I also keep my life in these sketchbooks. All the names of interesting typefaces, websites, blogs, people, phone numbers, email addresses, quotes are written there," he explains.

The unique aspect of these books and pages is that "they are free, rough and messy. They are for my eyes only so they are quick notations that only I have to understand. They are my concerns about letterforms. They are about type, language, and my shopping lists."

Pierre di Sciullo

Atelier Pierre di Sciullo is located in the Paris
suburb of Montreuil, France. His website
name (quiresiste.com), derives from his
publication *Qui? Résiste*, published in 1983,
and it has grown into a hothouse for fonts
and graphic design that he has created. He
is also an avid keeper of sketchbooks.

The book excerpted here was finished
days before he sent it in for this publication.
"I always have several sketchbooks in
progress," he says. "My purpose is to think
with my hands." In fact, he further notes that
with his sketches "I can see the different
stages of a project, or a repetition of a work
I have made before in order to understand
it better, or series of letters like a musician
doing his lines of notes."

The most unique aspects of his
sketches, he proclaims, are "timeliness and
sensuality. They can be viewed as part of a
series, but sometimes they can be viewed
for themselves, not like a former step of
something else." He also takes pride in
another key element: "Simplicity."

Dd

Porta
"b"

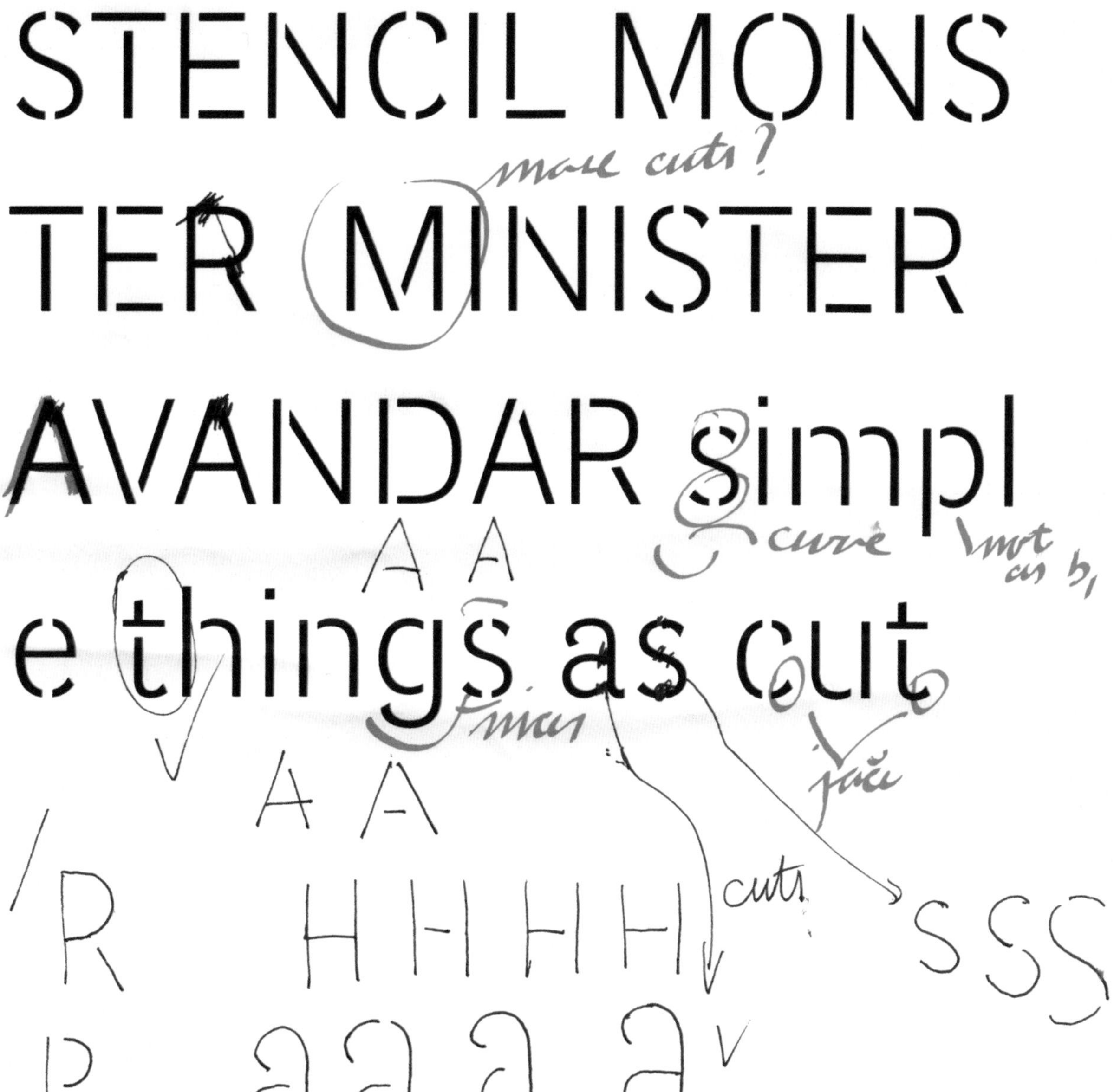

STENCIL MONS
TER MINISTER
AVANDAR simpl
e things as cut

more cuts?

curve *not as b,*

finer

jači

cuts

A A A
A A
R H H H H S S S
R a a a a

Nikola Djurek

Born in Zabok, northwest Croatia, Nikola Djurek runs the Typonine Font Foundry with offices in Croatia and the Netherlands, teaches at the University of Zagreb and the Academy of Art in Split and has designed Tempera, Tempera Biblio, Greta Display and Greta Grande (with Peter Bilak; see page 42), Brioni, and Amalia. He starts his process by making sketches "in the way that I prefer; it can be a different letter each time, but it's usually a lower-case letter, and then maybe two caps just to gauge the proportions. Sketches become an important part of my design process when making new typefaces."

The sketch opposite is for a type specimen for Brioni: "Brioni developed spontaneously from practice with a broad-nib pen, but the result is a hybrid of calligraphic influences and subtle manipulation of the stroke terminals that brings Brioni Text close to sans serif models. The concept was later translated to a higher contrast version, which is a more conventional text typeface. The result is a highly functional typeface family that is easy to work with and inviting to read."

The other sketches, from 2002 to 2009, represent typefaces that were experiments or are in development.

RIJEKA NAŠI

SPLIT MAKA

OSIJEK OPATJ

ZAGORJE t

BEDEKOVČI

ZADARSAK

E ZABOK RUDAr

s ka Zagreb

a Hrvatska

r Ko VŠČAN i

i n Ai J g a

gi NkaF

Dd

Franceso Dondina

Based in Milan, with an office in New York, Francesco Dondina founded Dondina Associati to create logos, books, packages, magazines, and websites. Typography is a particularly strong asset, and drawing type is a distinctly pleasurable activity. "I have kept sketchbooks for about as long as I can remember," says Dondina. "I've always drawn and have always made sketches; it's a daily tool that I use. The sketches usually refer to specific projects that I am working on at any given moment, though I do spend a lot of time thinking about and doodling typefaces."

Dondina sketches to capture an idea. "When I have an idea, I first draw it. Then I go back to develop and refine it. As I tend to think visually, when I have to design something I first have a mental visualization of it. The sketches enable me to crystallize the mental image. Most, therefore, are purposeful drawings that are finalized in a project."

Michael Doret

Michael Doret, Los Angeles-based hand-letterer and founder of Alphabet Soup, has held on to quite a lot of the sketches that he's done during a four-decade career. Looking back over Doret's work, and specifically over these sketches, he says it becomes clear how much he was influenced by growing up in Brooklyn near Coney Island, the Brooklyn Dodgers, and Times Square. "There's nothing subtle about what I do, and it is all pretty much reflective of my love for low-brow signage, storefronts, billboards, sports ephemera, old movies, and anything and everything related to mid-century American pop culture. I can't help myself, and I can't keep these themes from bubbling to the surface."

Some artists create sketches that can stand on their own as works of art. "I do not believe that mine fall into this category," Doret says, "as they are all roughly drawn stand-ins for work that is intended to be much more tightly rendered. Perhaps what is distinct about them is the variety of approaches that I create for a single assignment that, although they are different, manage to fall into a single genre. If I try to look at my sketches as an outsider, I think that I might be struck by the endless design possibilities inherent in the twenty-six letters of the alphabet; that combining them with other design elements can open up endless varieties of imagery."

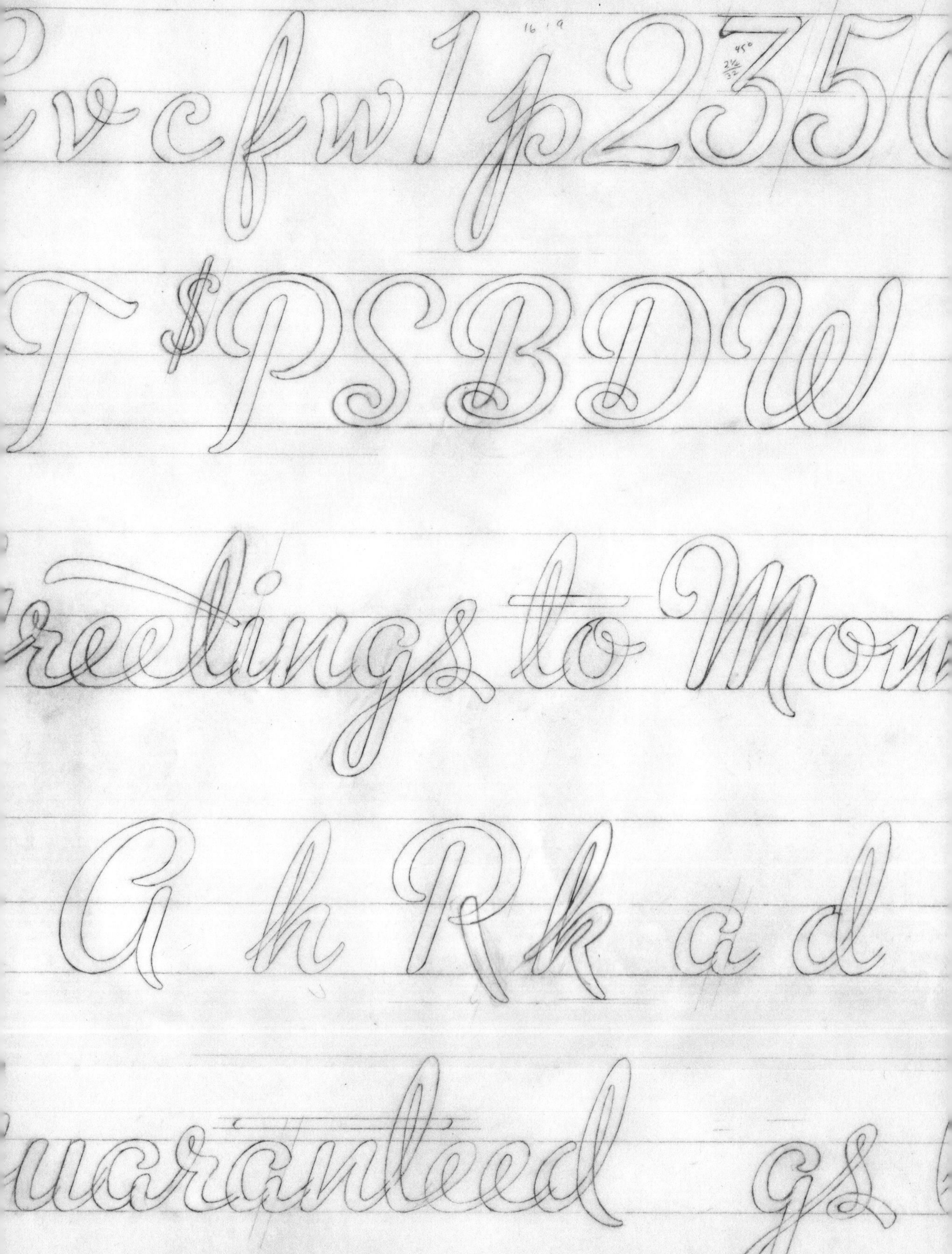

v c f w 1 p 2 3 5

45°
2½ / 32

T $ P S B D W

reetings to Mou

a h R k a d

uaranteed gs

932 923 942 940 917 940 914 937
over   over over   over

GR88FUL4u

Duarte Design

The folks at Duarte Design in Mountain View and Chico, California, are in the heartland of Silicon Valley. They state on their website: "We love whiteboards, sweet design, vegan cookies, bacon cheeseburgers, the afternoon regroup and the 4am idea. We believe in the power of a great story to move an audience and the power of an audience to change the world." On their blog they highlight notions of authenticity in business communications: "Presentations are boring because they are stripped of all humanness. Why do organizations present messages for human intake that are riddled with double talk, and lack authenticity?" You'd think with all the cookies and cheeseburgers and world-saving energy, they wouldn't have time to do much sketching.

Even though Nancy Duarte happily notes that "we're slammed with work," members of the studio have had time to make sketches of type experiments rooted in graffiti and wood type, among them Chris Francisco, Diandra Macias, Erik Chappins, Zach Rapatz, and Ryan Orcutt.

These may not be images and letterforms that connect with the business community, but they certainly have contact with the individual designers' unique lettering passions.

Ee

Emek

Born in Israel, Emek Golan is a Portland, Oregon-based music poster artist and lettering designer. He comes from an artistic family, so "I've had a sketchbook since my parents started keeping them for me, at the age of three. Actually my best sketchbooks are from when I was very young; my thoughts were more free, and I drew for fun," he says. And where have we heard that before?

Even today, Emek hints that he's not sure of the purpose of his sketches: "What is the purpose of any art?" But he then goes on to say, "To figure things out, to solve challenges, to answer questions, to document the past, to collect dust. I enjoy drawing immensely, but I never do it 'just for fun' any more. That's how I have been trained over the years – art is my life, but I always need a project first. All my projects start with a concept, then I figure out the style from there." It is a style known for its attention to detail and layers of sociopolitical content. Funnily, Emek doesn't know why he's saved the sketches shown here: "I don't know why, really. I'm just working things out."

THE FLAMING LIPS
EMMYLOU HARRIS
BEN FOLDS
STS9: SOUND TRIBE SECTOR
CAKE
ZAPPA PLAYS ZAPPA
MICKEY HART BAND
FEATURING STEVE KIMOCK &
GEORGE PORTER JR
KELLER WILLIAMS

THE POLYPHON

ROTHBURY

RPS

OF FLOWERS
OCTOBER 11

IF I WAS AS GOOD
AS YOU SAY YOU
ARE I WOULDN'T
TELL ANYBODY.

Ee

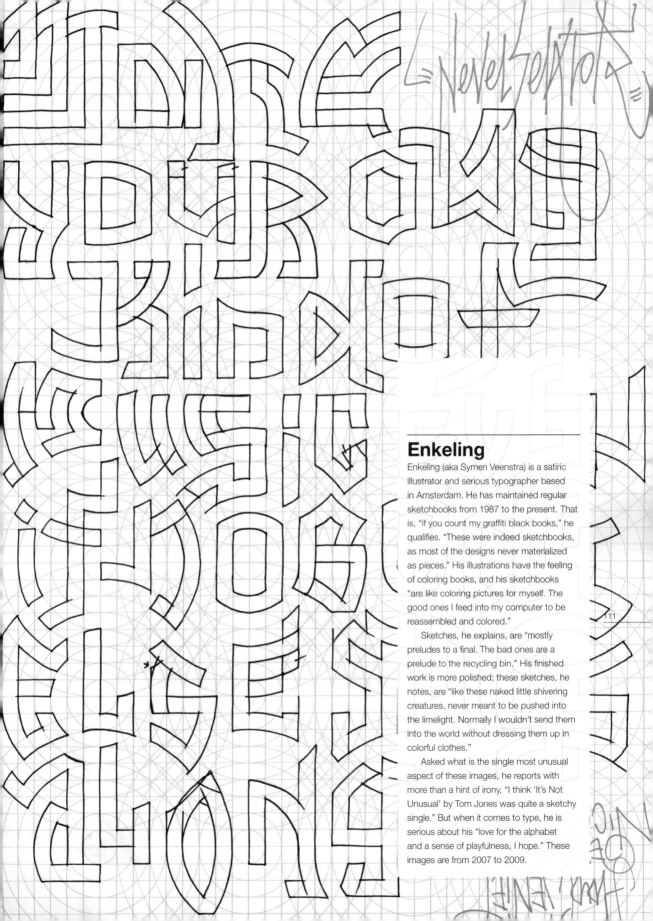

Enkeling

Enkeling (aka Symen Veenstra) is a satiric illustrator and serious typographer based in Amsterdam. He has maintained regular sketchbooks from 1987 to the present. That is, "if you count my graffiti black books," he qualifies. "These were indeed sketchbooks, as most of the designs never materialized as pieces." His illustrations have the feeling of coloring books, and his sketchbooks "are like coloring pictures for myself. The good ones I feed into my computer to be reassembled and colored."

Sketches, he explains, are "mostly preludes to a final. The bad ones are a prelude to the recycling bin." His finished work is more polished; these sketches, he notes, are "like these naked little shivering creatures, never meant to be pushed into the limelight. Normally I wouldn't send them into the world without dressing them up in colorful clothes."

Asked what is the single most unusual aspect of these images, he reports with more than a hint of irony, "I think 'It's Not Unusual' by Tom Jones was quite a sketchy single." But when it comes to type, he is serious about his "love for the alphabet and a sense of playfulness, I hope." These images are from 2007 to 2009.

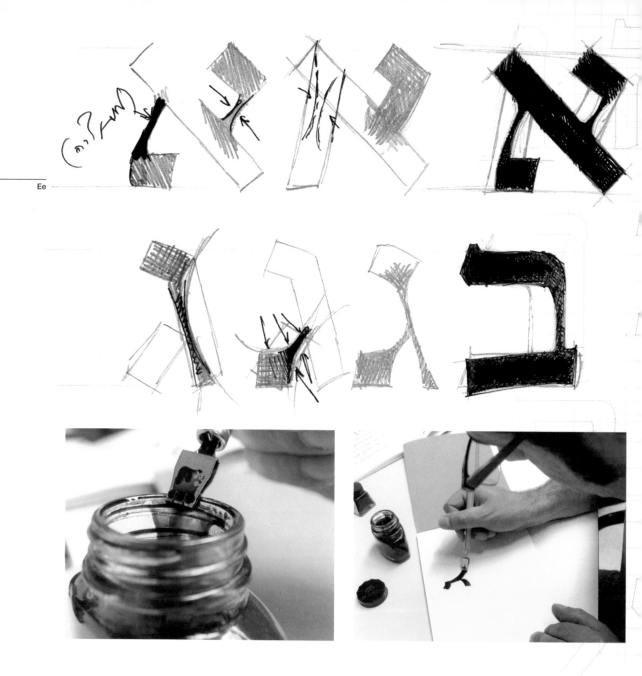

Oded Ezer

Oded Ezer is a typographic artist, logo and type designer. He is also a lecturer and a typographic experimentalist, based in Givatayim, Israel. Calligraphic Hebrew forms are his specialty. According to the blog design:related, his first monograph examined "the rich fusion of historic research, Israeli culture, calligraphy, classic typography, experimentation, storytelling, and science which come into play within his unique body of work." His métier is to bust the conventions of traditional letterforms within a three-dimensional space, sometimes with scientific precision.

Ezer has kept a sketchbook since he was a student at the Bezalel Academy of Arts and Design, "mainly to avoid forgetting my ideas." Some of his sketches are preludes to a final, others are musings without an end purpose. "The sketches are usually unpolished ideas only," he remarks. Some of these sketches, which were created between 2000 and 2010, are direct visual dialogues with ancient Hebrew manuscripts. But he also strives for what he calls "the search for the perfect visualization to a certain idea." That can be 1,000 years old, or from yesterday.

אבדהוז

חטיכךל

מםנןסע

פףץצקר

שת ׃

Le Be

David →

1506

ספר תהלים

12

מֵכִין הָרִים בְּכֹחוֹ נֶאְזָר בִּגְבוּרָה ׃ מַשְׁבִּיחַ שְׁאוֹן

יַמִּים שְׁאוֹן גַּלֵּיהֶם וַהֲמוֹן לְאֻמִּים ׃ וַיִּירְאוּ יֹשְׁבֵי

11

קְצָוֹת מֵאוֹתֹתֶיךָ מוֹצָאֵי בֹקֶר וָעֶרֶב תַּרְנִין ׃

CASSIE MS. LLCIND
JON MI N
RYAN GE
DARBY KEITH
MARRIA FEERER
R R R R R
S S S R S R HO
THE R E BEAR HO
N today NI T CE I B
is the
day
ER BEA T S BEAR
Pau Ile

Ff

Ryan Feerer

Texan designer Ryan Feerer is a veteran of New York's Funny Garbage, a design firm specializing in web design, where he worked with TeenNick, Nicktoons, and PBS Kids, among other entertainment companies for which his illustrative lettering is well suited.

"Right now I have about thirty sketchbooks that cover nearly the past six years of my life," he says. "I love flipping through them every once in a while for inspiration. I don't remember drawing the majority of the images, so it's always interesting."

Every logo, typographic layout, illustration, and most thoughts Feerer has, start out in his sketchbook. "I also do a ton of sketching that has little or no purpose other than entertainment. I don't play sports; I draw. I enjoy the aesthetic qualities of hand-drawn imagery, whether it be typographic or illustrative," he adds.

The purpose of his sketches is to put ideas and emotions on paper. "I consider it an art," he explains. "One day I'll die and someone will find hundreds of sketchbooks in my house. They'll be filled with drawings, designs, stories, thoughts, and grocery lists. Hopefully they'll think of them as a treasure. Maybe it'll make them happy. In one of my books I only write in Murk – an alphabet I made up; weird, I know."

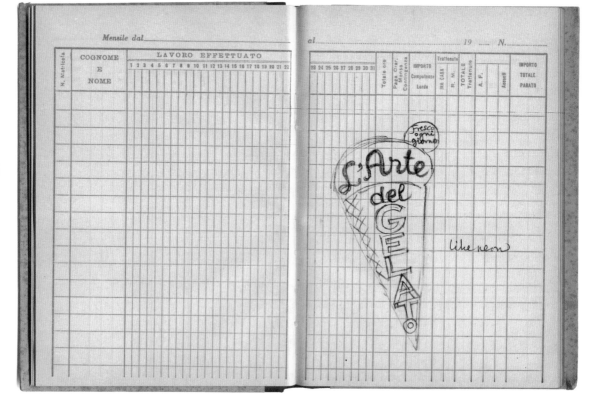

Louise Fili

New York designer and author Louise Fili is a maven for anything typographic, Italian, and food-related, individually and together. Once considered the doyenne of book cover design (with over 2,000 to her credit), her specialization shifted in the early 1990s to food packages and restaurant identities. A veteran collector of Italian typographic ephemera, she draws inspiration from Stile Liberty, Art Moderne and Futurist graphic design.

Fili carefully sketches out all her typographic concepts, working and reworking until the details and nuances are successfully achieved. But she doesn't always keep sketchbooks as repositories. Sketches can be produced on any paper, no matter what the weight. Common tracing paper works best, but envelopes, napkins, and oak-tag cards are sometimes just as effective. Of course, retaining them is not always easy, so Fili might tape them into the vintage address books or diaries she has obtained at Italian flea markets.

The example here, from 2009, shows a variation on a Deco-inspired logotype using one of her favorite scripts, for a New York gelataria, which makes the best *gelato* in the entire city (particularly the passion fruit and chocolate). This identity did not require many sketches since the idea was as fresh as the fruit used in their daily specials.

L'Arte del
GELATO™
Fresco ogni
giorno

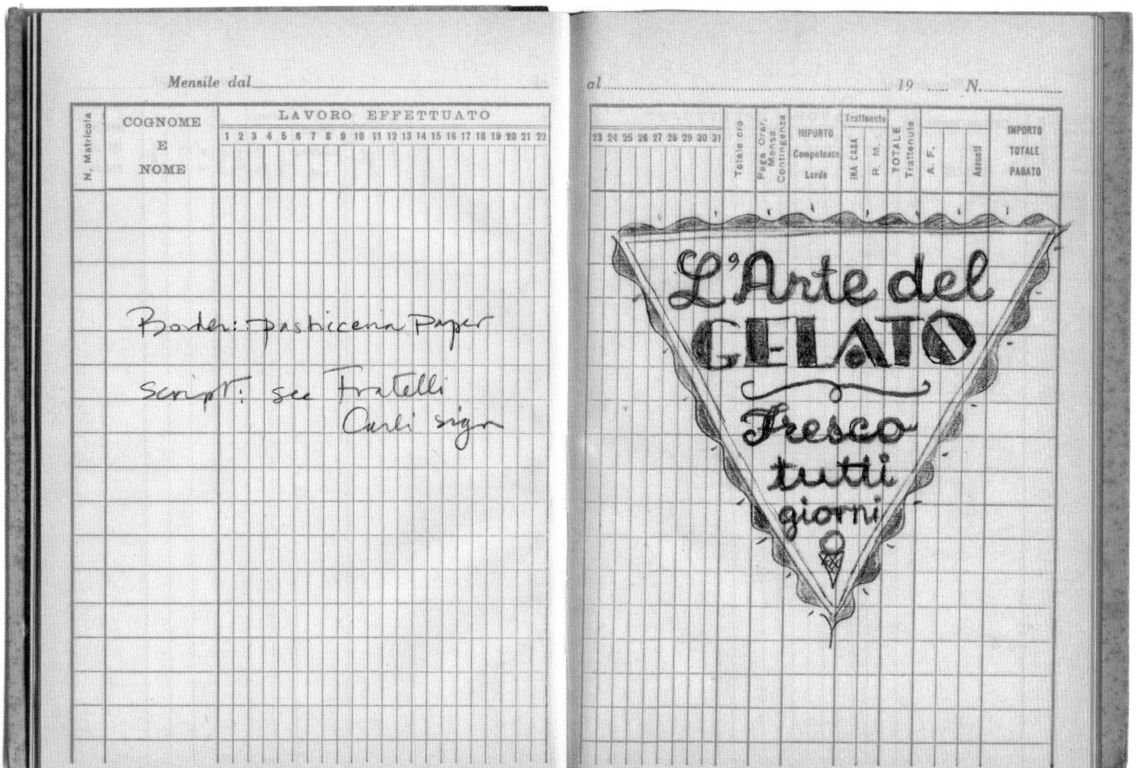
Mensile dal
al
19
N.
N. Matricola
COGNOME
E
NOME
LAVORO EFFETTUATO
1 2 3 4 5 6 7 8 9 10 11 12 13 14 15 16 17 18 19 20 21 22
23 24 25 26 27 28 29 30 31
Totale ore
Paga Orar. Mensa Contingenza
IMPORTO Competenze Lordo
Trattenute
INA CASA
R. M.
TOTALE Trattenute
A. F.
Acconti
IMPORTO TOTALE PAGATO
Border: pasticceria Paper
Script: see Fratelli
Curli sign
L'Arte del
GELATO
Fresco
tutti
giorni

Mark Fox

Mark Fox, a logo and icon designer, is located in San Francisco, where he collaborates with Angie Wang in the studio Design Is Play. Fox started keeping journals in college that comprised sketches, clippings, dreams, musings, and bad poetry – a record of his creative life at the time.

"My sketchbooks these days are similar – minus the bad poetry," he admits, "although they now include drawings by my kids. My sketches have various purposes: to record images I find interesting, to pay attention in a focused way, to maintain a facility with drawing, to problem-solve, to generate ideas, to imagine, to play with my children, etc."

Fox does not usually sketch without a purpose, "although that purpose may be non-commercial or even dubious! Peter Schjeldahl has written that 'drawing is thinking,' and I use the sketch as a form of thinking and weighing (as in evaluating or testing)." His sketches are more immediate and gestural than the final work. "I typically hand-ink my sketches to perfect them, to make them conform to a precise geometry," Fox explains. "When we can, we prefer to have the final piece letterpress-printed, screen-printed, or hand-painted as a human (i.e. imperfect) counterpoint to the obsessive precision. My sketches tend to rely on the principle of synecdoche: what can I clearly convey with the least amount of prompting?"

136

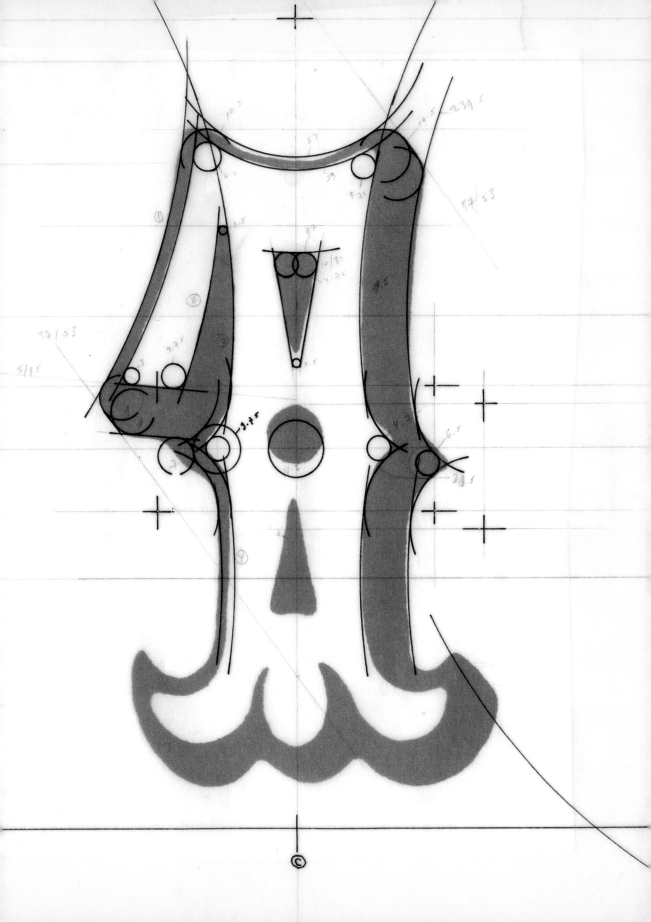

20'-6"

Tom Geismar

Tom Geismar is one half of the veteran duo Chermayeff & Geismar in New York (see also page 72), known for creating major identities for some of the most visible corporations and institutions in the world. Geismar is a logo designer *par excellence* and an exemplar of the Modernist tradition. Following methods he has maintained for decades, he says, "I almost always start with sketches; for me, it's the quickest way to get down ideas. I have always kept sketches for logos I've designed, mostly as a source of reference." And, of course, they often relate to a design problem that he needs to resolve. His

final work is precisionist to a fault, but sketches are essential. "For me, designing is a process. While I start with simple rough sketches, I then tend to develop some of the ideas into more and more complete forms, though still with pencil or marker on paper. Eventually these get scanned into the computer. Often the Illustrator drawings are then further studied and refined for form, color, etc."

Like most sketches, Geismar's "are a window into the artist's way of working, and sometimes his or her thought process." The images shown here span the period from the 1970s to 2009.

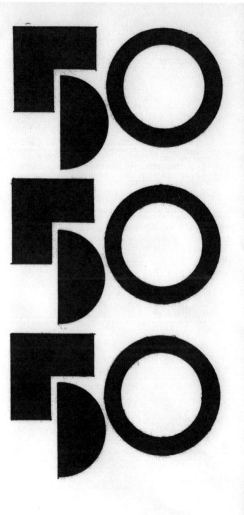

YES
WE
CAN

Gg

Tim Girvin

Seattle is where Tim Girvin, master calligrapher and typographer, creates his typographic and lettering magic. "I've been drawing and keeping journals and sketchbooks since the beginning of my career, which stretches back to the 1970s," he says.

"For me, the sketchbooks are always about curiosity," he adds. "And from that, exploring potential, in curious explication; and finally, it's about the moment, and the momentum – getting there. I'll use pretty much anything I can get my hands on, from a brush to an ink-dipped Victorian scribal tool, a stick, or a pencil, scribbled on anything, sometimes even patching that into the book. Journals, for me – sketchbooks – they're collages of life."

Girvin, the staunch formalist, says he actually savors drawing in a looser form. "Actually, I believe that the real energy of an idea finds life in sketching, because you're drawing around an idea; that looseness lends itself to finding the heart of the ideal. Energy is how that ideation works: the more you can work around that, the more vital it becomes – keep at it, and it can shine. For me, sketching really gets to the spirit of illustration, in an etymological context; lustration: to make something shine; that's what it is."

After opened up this downtown

ABCDEFG
HIJKLM
NOPQRST
UVWXYZ
1234567890
!&():;,.?/

SIMON AND GARFUNKEL

Simon

Milton Glaser

Milton Glaser was the co-founder with Seymour Chwast in 1954 of New York's groundbreaking Push Pin Studio. An illustrator, restaurant designer, and educator, he has designed display typefaces including Glaser Stencil, Hologram Shadow, Houdini, Kitchen, Sesame Place, Aint Baroque, Baby Teeth and Keepon Truckin, but each of them has left a distinct impression (or kiss, as hot metal typographers would say) on multiple generations. Glaser Stencil continues to be a viably fashionable face – one of many popular stencils on the market today.

Glaser always said he was "not a type designer," and that his typefaces only came into being as the product of graphic ideas applied to letterforms. Even so, Glaser's stylized type, with an emphasis on three-dimensionality, has had a lasting effect on the design of many subsequent display types; it combines Push Pin-era Deco motifs with conventions adapted from hand-painted signs, and are expressive of his illustration.

Here, in these sketches for a 1967 concert poster for Simon and Garfunkel, Glaser tries Babyfat (opposite) and Aint Baroque (above). In *Milton Glaser: Graphic Design*, he notes that Babyfat inspired his approach to the final poster: rather than the type following the example of the graphic, the reverse happened – the shape of the letters dictated the treatment of the figures.

Jonny Hannah

Jonny Hannah is an illustrator who, among other conceits, specializes in hand-lettering, often drawing upon Victorian styled typefaces. His home is in Southampton, England, "but I spend most of my time in an imaginary location," he confides; "downtown Darktown or Smithville."

His sketches "often end up as a final piece one way or another, but they sometimes act as a joke with no punchline. It can take six months to a year for them to see the light of day, depending on how quickly I look through that particular notebook again." Hannah professes not to take the sketches too seriously. "I don't care about

them. They can be as stupid or as sophisticated as the moment deserves. Charlie Parker played with a sense of abandon that few other artists have achieved in their final work. The only point where they cross over is when I paint. When I have a paintbrush, my devil-may-care side comes out, and I do just what I want. And for some reason, I don't mind exhibiting that side of me."

The starting point for his type sketches are often interesting words. "I love reacting to juicy prose or poetry or song lyrics. Whatever comes to my attention, via my iPod or external influences, from 'bring me my chariot of fire' to 'Rocket 88.'"

friday 27th march → double bill *
the Burns Project: Jazz in the
Scottish Dialect * the Euan Burton
Quartet with Phil Bancroft.
Saturday 28th March → double bill *
Ben Bryden Band *
John Randall Quintet *
* * Sunday 29th march *
John Lowrie
plus Paul
Towndrow
*

the 2nd Dumfries

*the → JAZZ ← 2009
CLAMJAMPHRIE

27th → 29th march

all events
are at So Below, 24 Castle Street,
Dumfries → Scotland * * *

www.dumfriesjazz.com ←

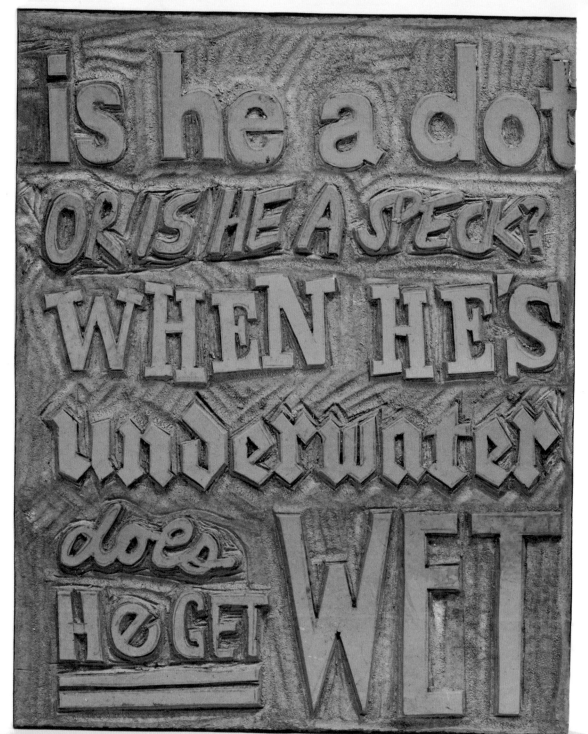

is he a dot
OR IS HE A SPECK?
WHEN HE'S
underwater
does
HE GET WET

Weekend Dirty

jobs in...

emerging media

MFA DESIGN THESIS GUIDE 08-09

Steve Haslip

New York-based English designer Steven Haslip declares that "the main purpose of my sketches is to visualize a design, no matter how rough or early on in the process, whether it be for a poster, logo, or type. I am also an avid doodler."

Typically, Haslip's sketches are used as part of his design process – "Draw first, compute later." Or, as shown here, make a woodblock first and last. "I still sketch everything that ends up on the computer – it's ingrained into the way I think through a problem. I make many sketches of the same thing until the idea takes form. It's very rare that the sketch ends up looking identical to the digital piece. It's also typically only done in one color."

He insists that the main theme of his sketches and sketchbooks is time. "I work quickly when I sketch to force myself to make decisions, even if they end up being the wrong ones. I feel like I have to get all the ideas out of my system and onto the page, especially the bad, so I can get to the good ones," he says.

(Logotype for IDPURE magazine)

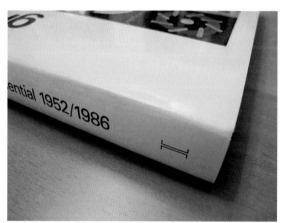

(Open book symbolic for IDPURE publishing)

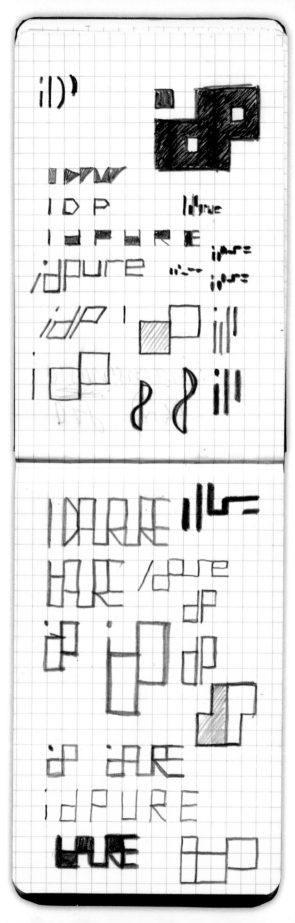

Thierry Hausermann

Thierry Hausermann, editor and designer of the Swiss design magazine *IDPURE*, recalls: "I learned in school to make sketches as a way to process my ideas. It is too bad that many students today are no longer doing this. Actually, I have different sketchbooks. Some books are more about concepts, ideas, or logos, and others are more about illustrations, doodles, and writing."

Hausermann uses the majority of his sketches for logo projects where he plays with basic elements like type, forms, or symbols. They are to "capture in the moment what could be a good idea, so that I can check later to see if I still think it's good. The purpose is not to make nice sketches, but more to remember. It is also about trying to work through possibilities and combinations to make sure a great visual aspect didn't get missed. Usually, I don't keep them."

Regarding his process, Hausermann notes, "I never know how I start. I feel uncomfortable in the starting process because I have no idea where I am going. I always find a way at the end." He enjoys seeing an evolution "from the most basic and classic ideas that anybody can have to the one you think is 'unique.'"

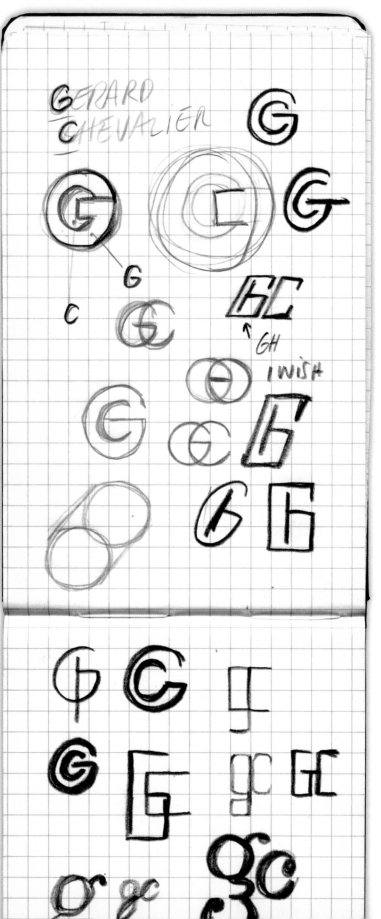

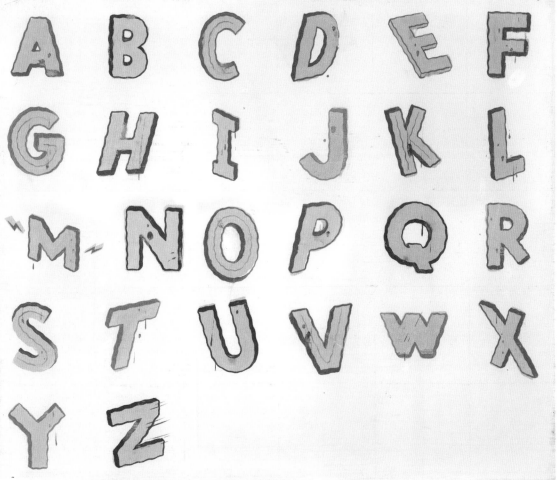

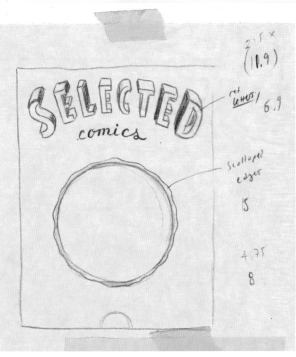

Ryan Heshka

Vancouver-based Ryan Heshka was born in Brandon, Manitoba and raised in Winnipeg at the end, he says, of the "lo-tech" era. He worked in interior design and animation before his present career as an illustrator of the macabre – with a special interest in hand-lettering on a monumental futuristic scale.

He has kept sketchbooks for twenty years and these are basically "idea catchers," he says. "Generally the sketches are direct, raw translations from what is in my head, without any polish." Thus, "often I will put down an idea that appeals to me, and then use it in a later painting or project. Although sometimes it can be years between the sketch and the final."

His letterform sketches have a rather carnivalesque aesthetic. "I like to think the color palette is unusual, or at the very least unique," he says. He might also add that the sketchbooks are where "creepy themes and styles tend to appear a lot."

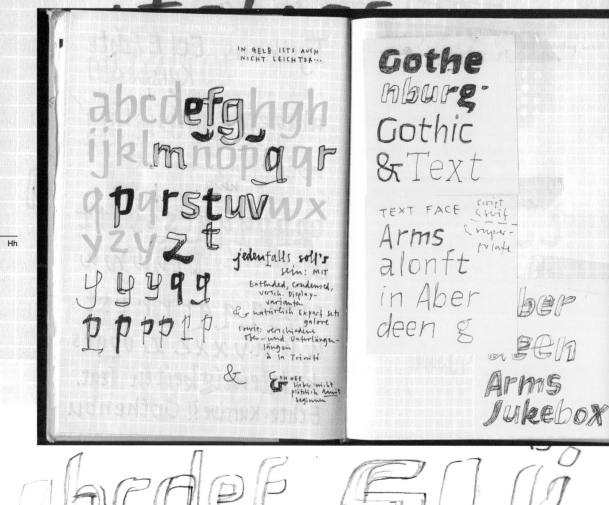

Benjamin Hickethier

German-born Benjamin Hickethier, a graphic designer currently living in Stavanger, Norway, has embarked on designing a typeface he calls Gothenburg. Although there is no finish yet, and it consists mainly of a concept and numerous approaches, sketchbook spreads, and single-letter investigations, there are sketches which, he says, "expand from a start towards an (aimed or not) finishing, maybe following some vague idea of a solution for a task, and trying out several possible paths to get there. And then there are sketches that could be summarized as joyful pastimes or maybe compared to improvisations in jazz, and then of course also sketches as studies of seen or imagined objects, the latter usually without an end purpose; in some cases those sketches might get used in solving design problems."

Hickethier had a sketching epiphany when his two sons turned old enough to hold a pencil and draw. "Spending time with them drawing, or watching them developing pictures, is just indescribably giving. They're so fantastic. And this experience has taught me a lot about my own sketching; about being more open and less expecting a certain result. Not to forget it is so much fun!"

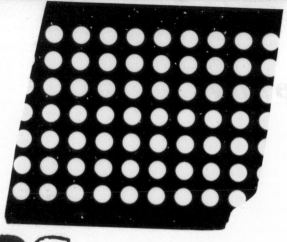

 ← slik?

LET'S MAKE IT LAST FOREVER

N P O D J j y

N æ e e

h [modular!

m n e p q

Hh

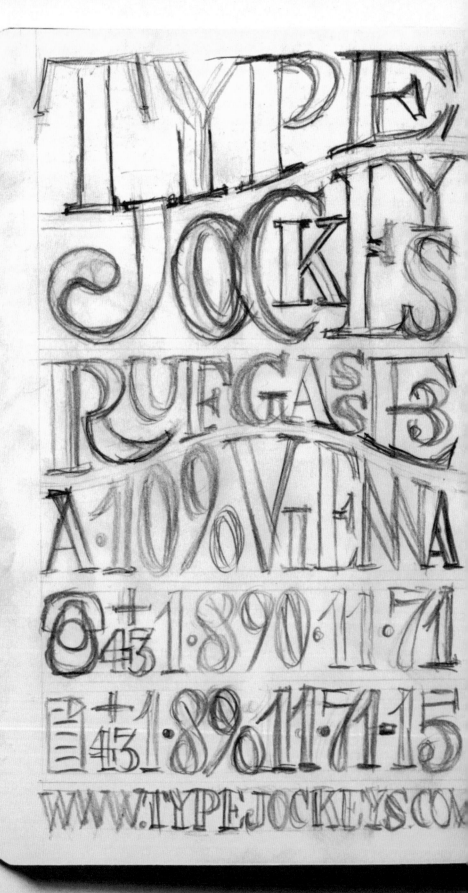

Michael Hochleitner

Michael Hochleitner, typeface designer, letterer, and co-founder of Typejockeys in Vienna, received an MA in typeface design at the University of Reading, UK, in 2007, but he's been an avid sketchbooker since he was a wee fourteen, when he started studying graphic design in Vienna. "I knew I was supposed to have a sketchbook," he says, as though resigned to his fate.

Sketching is not a burden. In fact, he explains, "It is easier for me to draw by hand. I can try out ideas quicker, and especially with letterforms the shapes get much more natural when I start by hand." Most of the time his sketches are the prelude to the computer design, "which is necessary to make our work reproducible. With the computer, obviously, it is much easier to manipulate forms and fine-tune them to an infinite level."

Hochleitner also notes, "Sketches to me are somehow 'more truthful' than the fine-tuned end product. The fact that a human being was the one producing it, is very clear and charming! Nevertheless, I'm a fan of perfection at the same time."

Ingeborg Roman | Ingeborg Bold

20/01/08

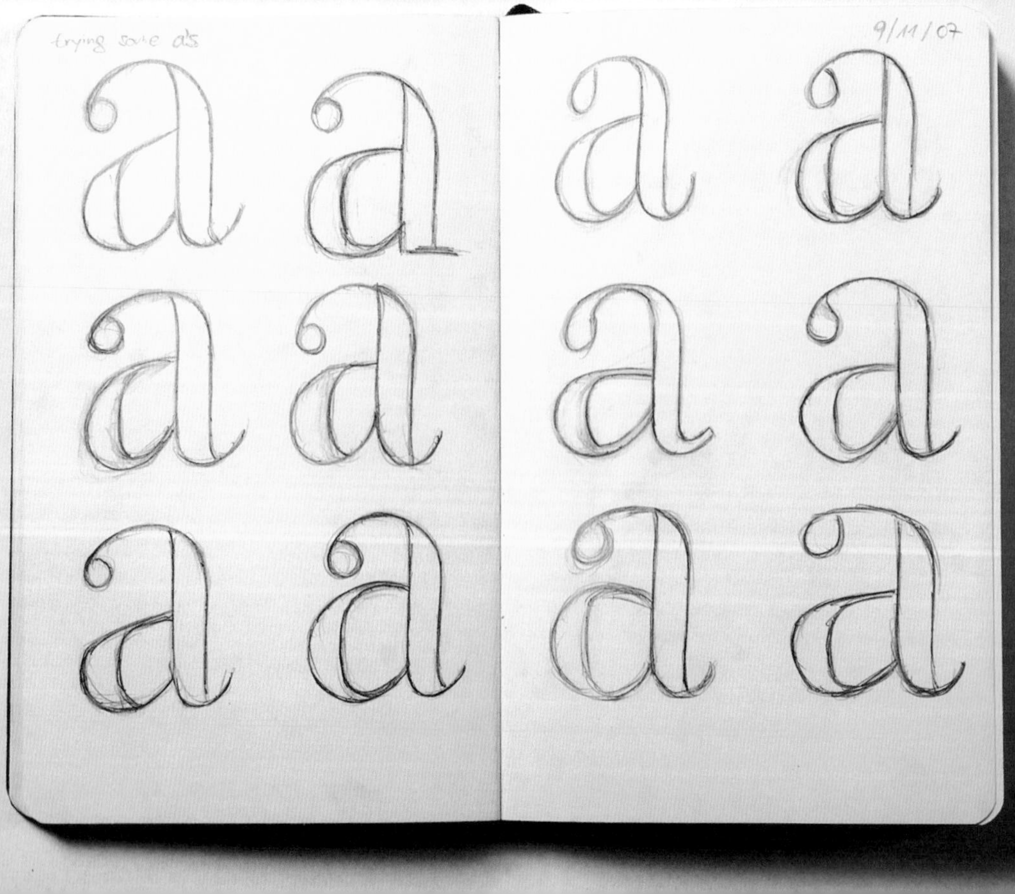

trying some a's

9/11/07

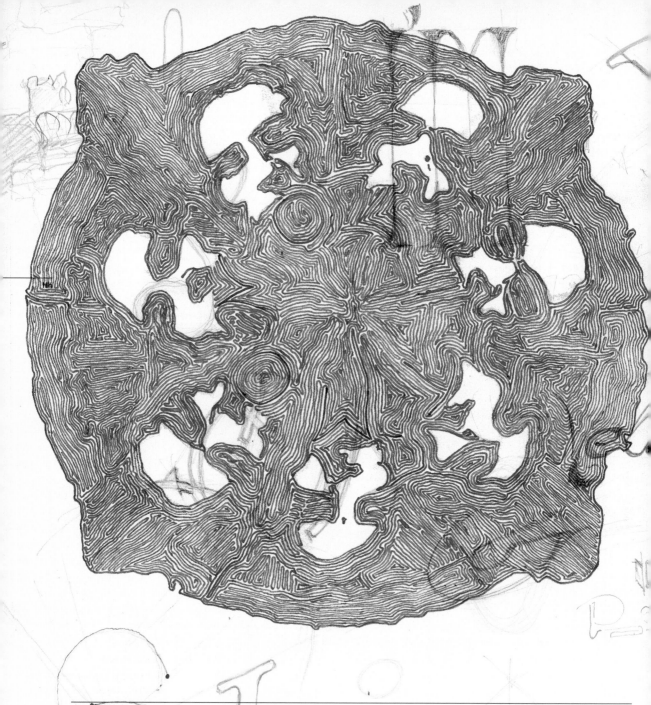

Ovidiu Hrin

Ovidiu Hrin from Timisoara, Romania, began sketchbook hoarding "in the beginning of my graphic design career, when I first felt the urge to keep track of my thoughts and interior ramblings," he reports. "As there were many crowded ideas and thoughts in my mind whirling around, keeping track of these was (then) my salvation. In time it transformed gradually into a playground, a place where I can be myself without caring about the 'mind-cargo.' Quite recently I've split it into different kinds of 'containers:' journal, sketchbook, design-process book, dream-record, and I am writing in all of them at the same time."

He says this documentation process could be a mixture of some of the following characteristics: "Self-reflection, de-coding how I work (internally), thirst for knowledge, trying to be a better person, the wish for growth and remaining open to inquiry. The only times I see the purpose behind all this is when I re-analyze my (past) self, and that process creates a purpose for the moment."

Hrin's sketches "grasp the moment," while the finished work adheres "to its predefined rules/limits. I usually try to encapsulate this 'moment' in the finished work. Therefore I like the finished work but I will always love the sketch."

Rian Hughes

London-based comics artist, letterer, and
design archaeologist Rian Hughes, known
for his published collections of graphic
ephemera, has kept sketchbooks since
before college. "Though I keep text notes
on my iPhone too," he qualifies in deference
to those who prefer high technology, "and
am prone to taking photographs that serve
as notes. It all feeds in."

Since he is so prolific, and apt to forget
essentials, he requires the sketchbook to,
as he says, "pin down an idea, even if in
note form comprehensible only to myself, for
later referral and development. I'll doodle the
essential features of a font to try and see if
it has any potential across the complete set
of character shapes. Only then do I boot up
Fontographer."

Sketches are always potentially
surprising: "I'm not sure why, but sometimes
the simplified essence of a sketch
communicates an idea more clearly than
the polished end result does. Though
sometimes the opposite is true; in pinning
down the essentials of a face in vectors it
can develop in interesting and unexpected
directions." Hughes's sketches from 2000
to 2010 shown here are experimental and
not particularly finished. "At this stage it's
all about the basic concepts, the loosest
parameters of the idea. Start with the
general and work towards the specific,"
he says.

Pedro Inoue

São Paulo, Brazil-based Pedro Inoue's work comes to life in digital form. "My first job was in Illustrator 7.0. I grew up surrounded by vectors and keyboard shortcuts. There was always the 'undo' command. A page is duplicated and two paths appear: all options are possible," he says. Sketchbooks are where he does artworks by hand: "They tend to have a more 'therapeutic' approach. I look again the next morning or a week after: maybe I haven't seen something that day, and the way I look into it changes – like my feelings and body temperature change every day."

As for his notebooks, "Most of the time I collect things, memories, thoughts, dreams I am afraid to forget – illegible letterforms that I scribble half asleep in the middle of the night." There are recurrent ideas, projects in progress; Inoue swears, "I will do them someday (like the short film of the suicidal mustard jar). I took a sketchbook from 2001 from the shelf and was amazed to see that the desperation I had then gave way to a much subtler tone. But the passions are mainly the same."

The images shown here are from 2007 to 2009.

KE
EPD
ANC
ING

TOCO
TU
BOCA

Erik T. Johnson

Erik T. Johnson, designer and illustrator in Minneapolis, Minnesota, is one of many who have been sketchbooking since high school. He says his main goal is to develop a lot of concepts for short comics, many of which never get realized. But with a dramatically drawn title he gets a chance to play with dynamic letterforms. Looking through his sketches, there are more typographical drawings than he would have expected: "I love that place where type and art intersect, and type drawings really help me establish the mood/thinking about a concept, whether I include them in a final piece or not."

Of course, after the sketch more has to be done – he has to fine-tune the degree of clean-up and finish – but "I like keeping my work loose in general; there is nothing precious about my sketches," he says.

Johnson's career as both an illustrator and graphic designer has its roots in a love of comic book vernaculars – which in their best forms become a seamless blend of drawings and drawn type (Winsor McCay's *Little Nemo*, George Herriman's *Krazy Kat*, Will Eisner's *The Spirit*, and Harvey Kurtzman's *Mad* are classic examples). "These sketches (though much cruder) really show the influences of that tradition," he notes.

Jj

1. WHAT? A HAT.

EXALTATIONS

OBSERVATIONS

UNRESOLVED INTERACTIONS THAT PLAGUE ME WITH GUILT

UNSPOKEN FEELINGS

FLORAL ARRANGEMENTS

Pro...

QUESTION
WILL WE D...
WILL WE EA...
WILL THE...
WILL WE G...
WILL THE...

FEA...
HOP...

SPINOZA?

HOME

BREAKFAST
STARING
COFFEE CAKE
OBITS

LIST OF OTHER DESIRES

FEELINGS

Dead Mummy

The Pri... of UNCERTA...

2. FORGET it.

YOU NEVER KNOW

DESPERATE DESIRES

DO

LONGINGS
YEARNINGS
AFFLICTIONS
PANGS of REGRET
REMORSE

NOD HEAD
BUY STRING
CATALOG
ALL THINGS
DANCE IN OTHER COUNTRY

BEAUTY

WO... OF U...

VALUED OBJECTS
LUX BOBBY PINS

THINGS TO DO
PROMENADE

RUN UP and DOWN the HALL
SHAKE HEAD. HTS

RECENT PURCHASES

DREAM WHIP PUDDING

* PURCHA...

HOURGLASS
INDIAN TUNIC
HAT
HAT
BOOK ON DAFFODILS
ENVELOPES
30 MOCHA CREAM CAKES

SI...
OB...
EL...
·SI...
·TH...
·WA...
·ST...
·SI...

PLEASURES, DELIGHTS.
HILARITY. MIRTH.

FLIP HAIR. SNAP FINGERS.

STOPPING TO THINK
LAST VESTIGE OF THOUGHT
INTERRUPTIONS /
DIGRESSIONS

FASHIONABLE ATTIRE

SPOON

LOOKING TIP TOP
ELEGANTO and DASHING

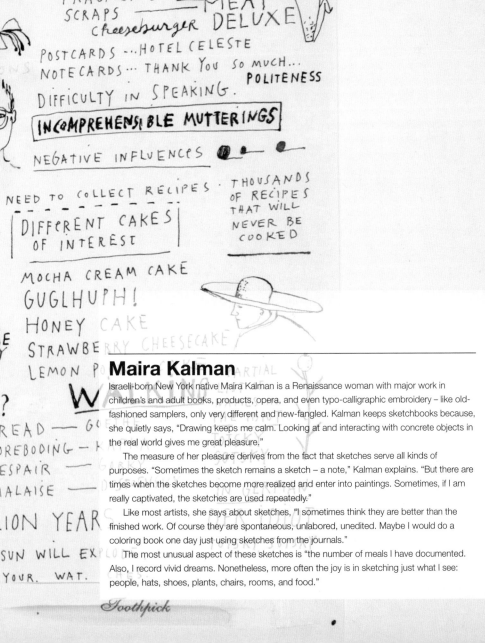

VALUABLE THINGS

PRACTICING OF MUSICAL INSTRUMENTS

PIANO
FLUTE
ETC.

THE PRINCIPALS

JHS 141 - MISS COVINO
M+A - HIGH SCHOOL
MR. WECHSLER
ASST PRINCPAL
~~MR. STOOPACK~~

de

DUEL?
ALAD SANDWICHES?
BLOW UP?
WALK?
OOK RIGHT?

ILL
OF
T

ished
geRe

s

RABLE
EAUTY

anny Kaye
ed Astaire

UVENIRS

NG

TE BOREDOM?

ETTING UP
G
G

TOOTHPICK

MISTAKES.

COLLECTIONS
MOSS and SPONGES
NOTEBOOKS
DIARIES
JOURNALS

FRAGMENTS
SCRAPS ——— cheeseburger
MEAT DELUXE

3. FORGOTTEN. FORGOTTEN THEN
FOUND UNDER BEDS, IN DRAWERS, IN DUSTY CLOSETS,

ZEPPELIN

POSTCARDS ··· HOTEL CELESTE
NOTECARDS ··· THANK YOU SO MUCH···
POLITENESS

DIFFICULTY IN SPEAKING.

INCOMPREHENSIBLE MUTTERINGS

NEGATIVE INFLUENCES

NEED TO COLLECT RECIPES
· THOUSANDS OF RECIPES THAT WILL NEVER BE COOKED

DIFFERENT CAKES OF INTEREST

4. MOCHA CREAM CAKE
GUGLHUPH!
MOCHA MOROSE MONEY
HONEY CAKE
STRAWBERRY CHEESECAKE
LEMON P

DREAD — G
FOREBODING — H
DESPAIR
MALAISE ——

5. BILLION YEAR
THE SUN WILL EX
. SET. YOUR. WAT.

Toothpick

Maira Kalman

Israeli-born New York native Maira Kalman is a Renaissance woman with major work in children's and adult books, products, opera, and even typo-calligraphic embroidery – like old-fashioned samplers, only very different and new-fangled. Kalman keeps sketchbooks because, she quietly says, "Drawing keeps me calm. Looking at and interacting with concrete objects in the real world gives me great pleasure."

The measure of her pleasure derives from the fact that sketches serve all kinds of purposes. "Sometimes the sketch remains a sketch – a note," Kalman explains. "But there are times when the sketches become more realized and enter into paintings. Sometimes, if I am really captivated, the sketches are used repeatedly."

Like most artists, she says about sketches, "I sometimes think they are better than the finished work. Of course they are spontaneous, unlabored, unedited. Maybe I would do a coloring book one day just using sketches from the journals."

The most unusual aspect of these sketches is "the number of meals I have documented. Also, I record vivid dreams. Nonetheless, more often the joy is in sketching just what I see: people, hats, shoes, plants, chairs, rooms, and food."

ABCDEFG
HIJKLMNOP
QRSTUVWXYZ
vwxyzabcdefgh
ijklmnopqrstu

Kk

Jeffery Keedy

Los Angeles-based type designer and design educator Jeffery Keedy (aka Mr. Keedy) says, "Like most designers, I have usually had a few sketchbooks going at once. But when I started designing typefaces I switched to single sheets of 8½" × 11" tracing paper. Since I was often working with laser print proofs from the computer and Xerox copies from old type catalogs, it made sense to keep all the materials together in one folder."

The sketches help Keedy see what he is thinking. "And they show me why most of what I am thinking is lame," he confides. "It is mostly a process of elimination but I also let myself wander and sometimes go far off topic, so it is fun and not all bad news. I rarely try to solve technical problems on paper; that is mostly done on the computer."

Keedy's sketches are not for "public consumption," he insists, although they are reproduced here. "They are not presentation drawings, they are for my use only. They are a mess, complete with tea stains and drawings on both sides of the paper in random order. They are a means to an end. They are not commemorative drawings of successful forms that look great and are reassuring. I look for that in the final work."

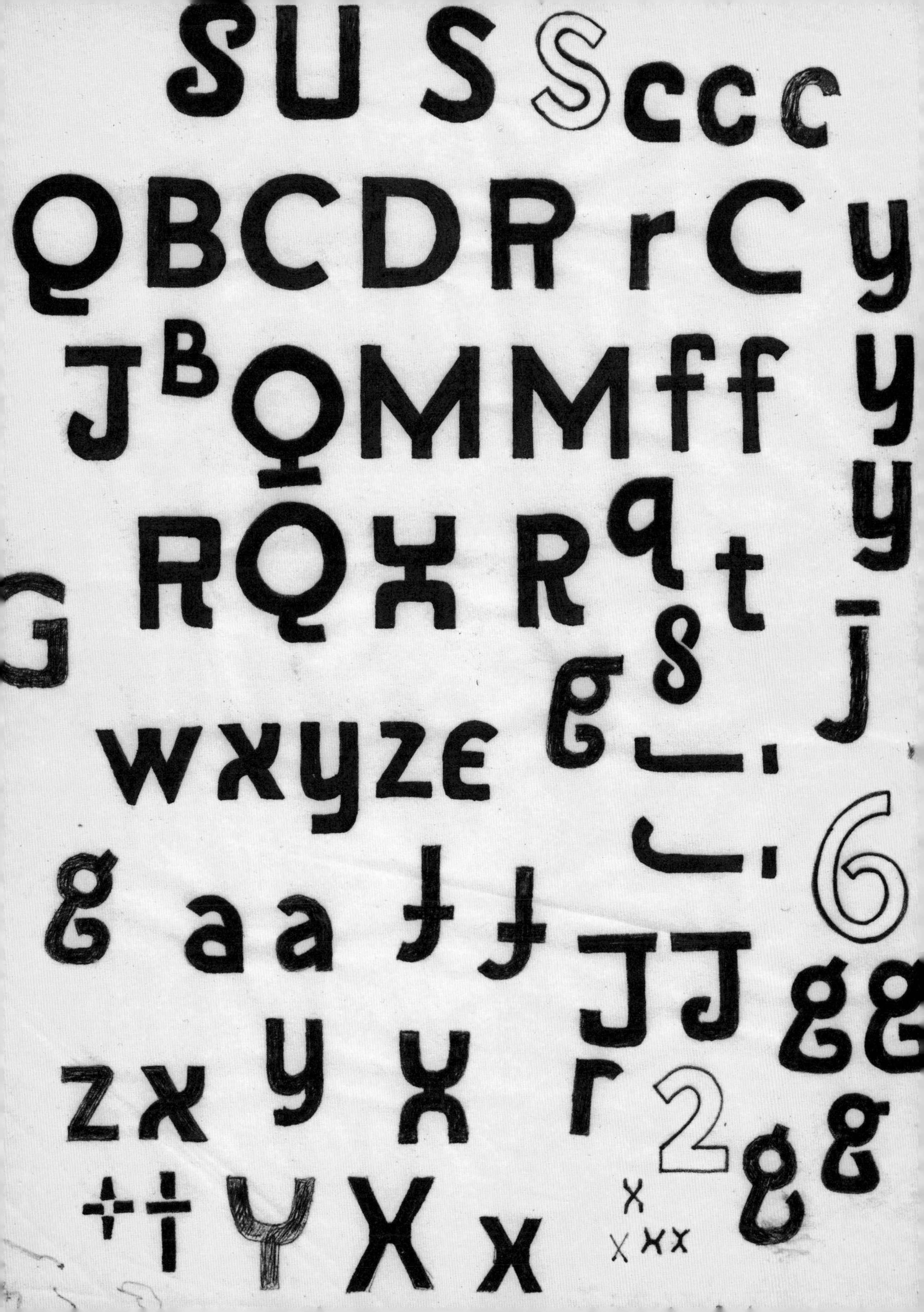

Viktor Koen

Greek-born, Israeli-trained, New York-based photo illustrator and letterer Viktor Koen uses sketchbooks "mostly for scribbling and crudely composing versions of ideas for illustrations, until I am satisfied and move to the screen. I also like working on type proportions, logos, and layouts in my sketchbook before choosing specific typefaces or sizes."

His books are made up of "mix and match" combinations, "and sarcasm, as I try to resolve problems through unlikely combinations of parts from opposites in order to get a point across," he says. "I also collect scraps of images I am attracted to without knowing why. My photography works in much the same way – until things click together in mysterious ways in this crazy thing we call commercial art."

Sketches and finals couldn't be more distant: "My sketching is a mixture of stick figures, hieroglyphics, esoteric doodling, and coffee stains – rarely understood by man or beast. The end result (and strength) of my published work is communication and visual impact."

Koen's sketches, some of these going back to the 1980s, "are perishable assets – working digitally has taken a crippling toll on my bare hand skills. I am so envious of my graduate students who effortlessly sketch away in class. Did I say envy? Hate and jealousy is what I meant."

Kk

18+

Verdge

Verdge

slaverhouse

Verdge

Verdge

```
70:      (714u,1676u) --
71:      (830u,1616u) --
72:      (830u,552u) --
73:      (950u,545u) --
74:      (950u,500u) --
75:      (700u,500u) --
76:      (700u,1489u) --
77:      (674u,1502u) ..
78:      (590u,1358u) ..
79:      (515u,1210u) ..
80:      (437u,1028u) ..
81:      (377u,858u) ..
82:      (330u,685u) ..
83:      (311u,587u) ..
84:      (300u,500u) --
85:      cycle;
86: endchar;
87:
88: beginchar("i",430u#,1745u#,0u#);
89:    fill
90:      (180u,500u) -- % 1
91:      (180u,1525u) --
92:      (26u,1410u) --
93:      (5u,1442u) --
94:      (310u,1710u) --
95:      (310u,552u) -- % 2
96:      (430u,545u) --
97:      (430u,500u) --
98:      cycle;
99:    fill
00:      (250u,1840u) .. % 3
01:      (214u,1847u) ..
02:      (186u,1872u) ..
03:      (167u,1908u) ..
04:      (161u,1946u) ..
05:      (169u,1992u) ..
06:      (185u,2025u) ..
07:      (217u,2053u) ..
08:      (255u,2064u) ..
09:      (292u,2055u) ..
10:      (318u,2032u) ..
11:      (338u,1995u) ..
12:      (344u,1953u) ..
13:      (339u,1911u) ..
14:      (318u,1871u) ..
15:      (290u,1848u) ..
16:      cycle;
17: endchar;
18:
19: beginchar("j",420u#,1745u#,455u#);
20:    fill
```

Handwritten annotations:
950, 565 --
950, 520 --
700, 478 -- --
180, 478
430, 565
430, 520

Andrej Krátky

Andrej Krátky, a Czech type designer based in Bratislava, Slovakia, has kept all the drawings and printouts shown here for more then twenty years. These original drawings for the typeface Nara, he notes, were "intended as a master for a titling photo-composition device." This project originated as his student thesis at the Academy of Arts, Architecture and Design in Prague, and continued for several years.

"The process started out old-fashioned – drawing all letters by hand in ink," he recalls. "Later I used Metafont to digitize the typeface and to create a slanted italic version. There was no graphical interface available to design typeface at that time, so I had to develop my own technique. I used a simple hand-made digitizer (a piece of glass with a transparent 'millimeter paper') to measure and write down all the coordinates of points on paths. From 1992 I was able to convert the resulting outlines into a PostScript-based Fontographer system, but I did not finish the work then. In 2005, typographer and editor Peter Bilak (see page 42) initiated new thoughts about the design and he helped me, together with type designer Nikola Djurek (see page 94), to finalize the font and release it under his Typotheque library."

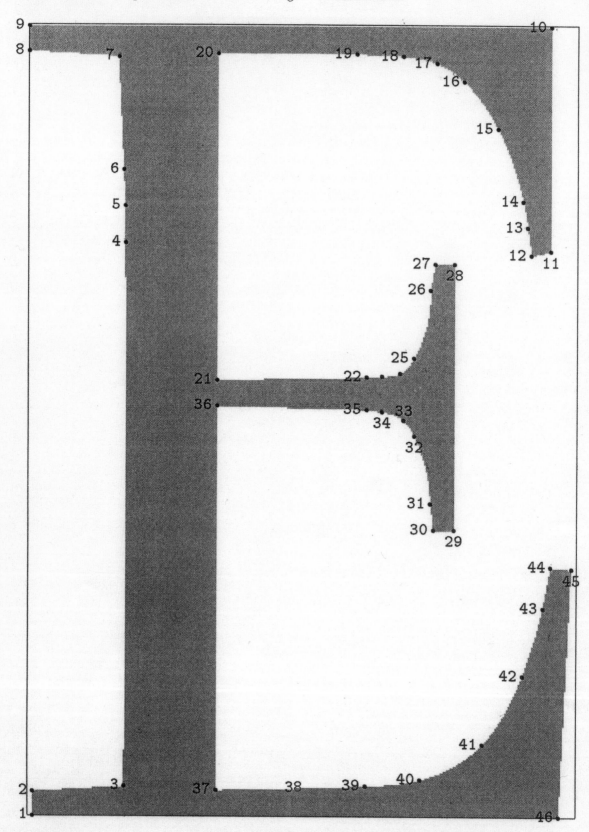

Tom Lane

Tom Lane, also known as Ginger Monkey, is based in Bristol, England. He is a designer, illustrator, and maker of things, including letterforms, for the arts and media, advertising, publishing, and social sectors. "I imagine I began sketching pretty late compared to most in this area of work – I didn't start getting into design, illustration, and typography until my early twenties," Lane explains.

Increasingly, he reports, his sketches are becoming the cornerstone of his process. "I've started to leave the computer completely behind in some cases, or use it simply as a finishing tool." This is probably because "I aim for a strong emotive response from an audience when they see my work. I feel the little imperfections, rougher edges, or general texture to sketches and hand-crafted work leave a little bit of me in the piece and the viewer picks up on that."

Lane calls this his "very rough, get-an-idea-down sketchbook." Some of his sketches are laid out in detail with measurements and some are simply laissez-faire. "At the time these were made (2009–10) I was still finding my feet with hand-lettering. Now, I'm drawing type all the time and have a pretty clear process. In these sketches you're seeing a cross-section of my education into drawing type, my learning through experimentation and discovery."

TVA AA
REVUE LE TRÈFLE
nouvelle
REVUE
FABRIQUÉE &
imprimée
À L'ANCIENNE

Jean-Baptiste Levée

Jean-Baptiste Levée is a type designer and typographer who lives in Paris and Montréal – but mostly in Paris. He designs typefaces and develops fonts for brands, corporations, and publishers. There are multiple goals for keeping his books – "To avoid getting bored during lectures and conferences is the main kick. But I also do it to empty my head of concepts and ideas; both to evacuate and to fix them on paper. It is also helpful to draw a shape by hand that I cannot get right with the computer."

Sketching mostly does not have any direct connection with his work. "I have been trying to use it to search for some italics for a roman I have designed, for instance, but so far it has never proved useful," he admits. "The sketches do not refer to anything other than themselves, although monograms or logotypes sometimes start in my sketchbook. It is the quickest tool I have to experiment with letter combinations, visual type tricks, rotations, etc."

He claims not to have "standards or expectations – the sketches can be as clumsy as they want, as long as I get the idea right."

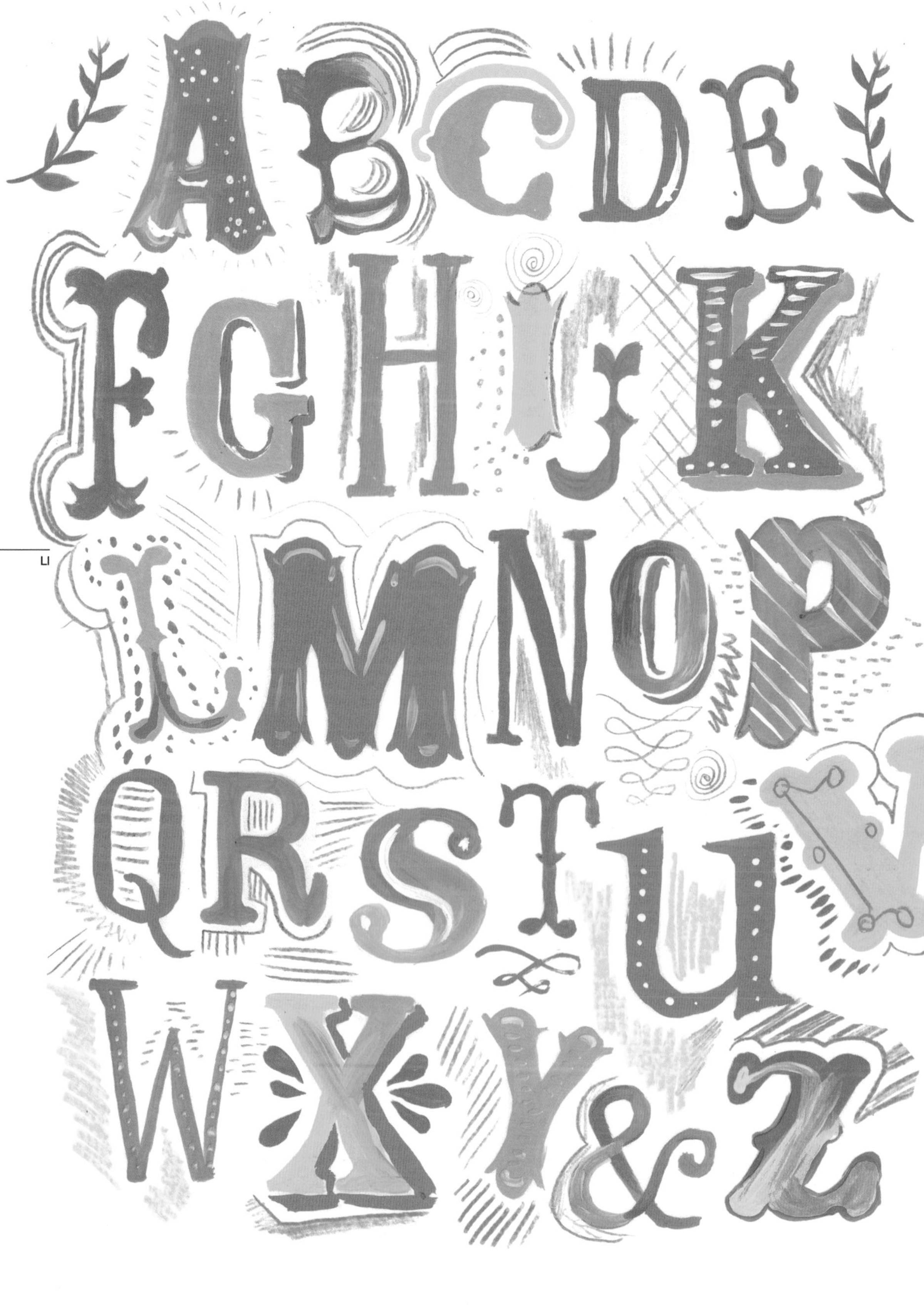
ABCDE
FGHIJK
LMNOP
QRSTUV
WXY&Z

Katie Lombardo

Katie Lombardo (aka Katie Daisy) calls herself "a wandering artist whose home is the prairie." She lives "between the Smoky Mountains and pure bliss," according to her website.

Originally from a small farm in Illinois, she is inspired by rural life. "Ms. Daisy makes her way by enjoying simple country pleasures such as a sweet goldfinch song, swimming in lakes, canoe trips that creep into the night and sipping chamomile tea with honey," her site reveals. Since studying at the Minneapolis College of Art

& Design, Lombardo has worked for clients such as Target, HGTV, and American Greetings.

Her sketches are as free and "blissful" as her voice. And her finishes are not much different from the sketches. The letterforms she prefers are soothing versions of nineteenth-century woodtypes, painted and watercolored with pastel tones and happy doodads. In fact, there are quite a few daisies integrated throughout her letters and words.

Yellow

KATIE LOMBARDO

FLOW

HOW DOES YOUR GARDEN GROW?

LAO TZU

Introduction

AUROBINDO

LOOK

SUNDAY

RAMANA MAHARSHI

Matt Luckhurst

Canadian Matt Luckhurst, a designer and letterer based in New York, says, "I didn't want to draw for a long time – my mom couldn't force me into an art class. It wasn't until high school and I was introduced to graffiti that my imagination was sparked. From there it was a prolific production of sketches to try to one-up my friends."

"I have a notoriously bad memory," Luckhurst notes, "so I always have something to draw on. They serve as a memory bank for me as well as being the first place I go when I start a project." He develops paintings and personal work from flipping back through his books.

"The most unique thing about these sketches is the lack of intention inherent in them," he adds. In fact, "sketches don't need to have an intent, other than to be sketches. Not to say they can't, but it is novel to have a place to let the mind and hand wander."

Luckhurst asserts that "nothing is ever unfinished in a sketchbook" – an interesting and contrary notion. "Every stroke is complete until a pencil finds it again. Things are allowed to grow organically and the page can grow and change as it pleases – I have terrible handwriting and I revel in a lack of organization."

The audience
They need,
what They want

(again)

WATCHMEN

reinterpretation of magical symbols

JOHN

art = magic

borders

fields and m

transformative force,
not entertainment

having same
thoughts at
same time

words are magic

Alan moore

Kim Gordon
not a mu

music = art

mainstream infiltrat

CALIFORNIA
LIGHT

sonic
youth

super fine thin lines

POP
GLOSSY

James ensor

pixies

consuming
creating

medical mas

DIY

A

Relax

it's OK

JUNK

stateless society

joy of pure thinking

kraftwer

obscenity of c

SLAVoj Žižek

common person produc

Lady MACbeth

bloody hands

guilt

J.G. ballard

manism

nothing to lose

Jim Morrison

momorab conclusions

cabaret

esert

death

THE Hermit

I'm interested in the man watching TV,
not the man making the programs

personal myt

antichrist

tim burton

part human

part animal

sol

Ludwig
wittgenstein

macabre wit

part plant

rand Russell

watching people watching art

Learn to forget

JOHN BALDESS

conceptual

BAUHAUS

Kubrick

Ron Cobb

alien

dutch concept

WHY the things are the way they are

Aleksandar Maćašev

Aleksandar Maćašev was born in Bečej, Yugoslavia, and graduated from the Faculty of Architecture at the University of Belgrade. A designer and typographer, he works in a variety of disciplines. Most of the time his sketching is visual play with no purpose: "An old typeface catches my eye, usually from some movie credits or a street sign. Or I want to note something down, but I also want to add some graphic quality to it – a quote, a thought, or a name that I want to remember. I often use hand-drawn slides when I give lectures and presentations. They offer a lively contrast to the usual computer-generated type."

Maćašev says all of these sketches are finished. "Let's define a sketch," he posits. "Sometimes sketches are used to find a solution, or they can also be graphic pieces that have sketchy qualities. These tend to be finished work, where I consciously decide to keep the unfinished, sketchy quality." In fact, he says many sketches are more finished than not. "It's funny when you look at a lot of recently published books of working sketches. They all look quite cool and polished. Artists and designers seldom publish their really messy working sketches that show the process of making things."

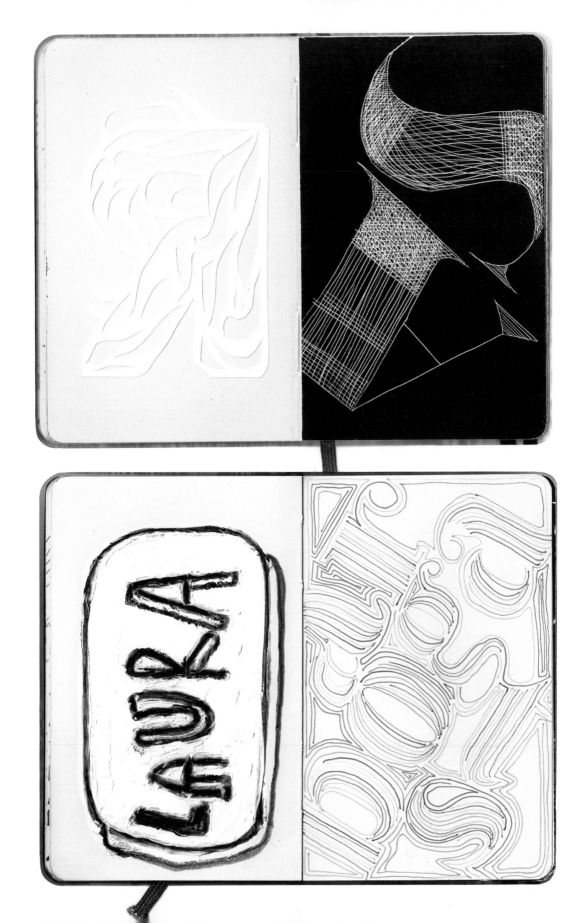

Mm

Ross MacDonald

Ross MacDonald, an illustrator and proprietor of a small but well-endowed letterpress and woodtype business called the Brightwork Press in Newtown, Connecticut, makes sketchbooks out of his throwaways and type scraps. He says, however, that he was sketching and doodling from an early age: "I used to draw in the margins of my school notebooks (and textbooks). Around grade three, I started cutting composition books in half so I could carry one in a pocket."

His type sketches are the first steps of designing, "trying to work out how everything goes on the page. They are a quick way of trying different approaches and versions, though lots of times the sketch will look great, but it won't work when I go on to try it." The most satisfying aspect of his sketchbooks is the artifact-ness of the materials. MacDonald makes props for movies (books, cards, etc.), often with historical patinas. His sketchbooks are the artless artifact versions of these.

THE GOOD THE BAD & THE UGLY

THE
GREAT
BIG
DESERT
EXCURSION

THE GREAT
BIG
DESERT EXCURSION

THE DE GREAT
BIG
DESERT
EXCURSION

THE DE GREAT
BIG
DESERT
EXCURSION

Richard McGuire

New York-based illustrator, comics artist, and creator of comic, noir animation Richard McGuire is very philosophical about sketching: "The purpose of sketching is to evoke," he says. "You start with a vague idea, this little seed, and then you have to clarify and clarify it, and bring whatever it is into the world and make it real. You are hunting the right side of the brain, or your subconscious, or some collective consciousness; you are trying to pull a rabbit out of the hat."

Drawing is largely "problem solving," he adds. "The end purpose depends on the project. I've scanned sketches into the computer and redrawn them with Illustrator if I need it to be precise. More recently, I've been using rough sketches as my 'finished' work, sometimes scanning and manipulating them a bit with Photoshop, but I've been appreciating the rough immediacy of a hand-drawn line, or a painted line."

The 2008 images shown here were designed for a record sleeve for McGuire's band Liquid Liquid. "I was attempting to create type that was inherently rhythmic-looking, trying to reflect the sound of the band. The end result went in a different direction – the type I made was much simpler, hand-painted, extremely easy-to-read block letters, white on a black background."

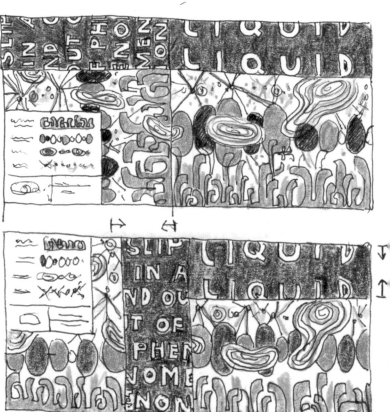

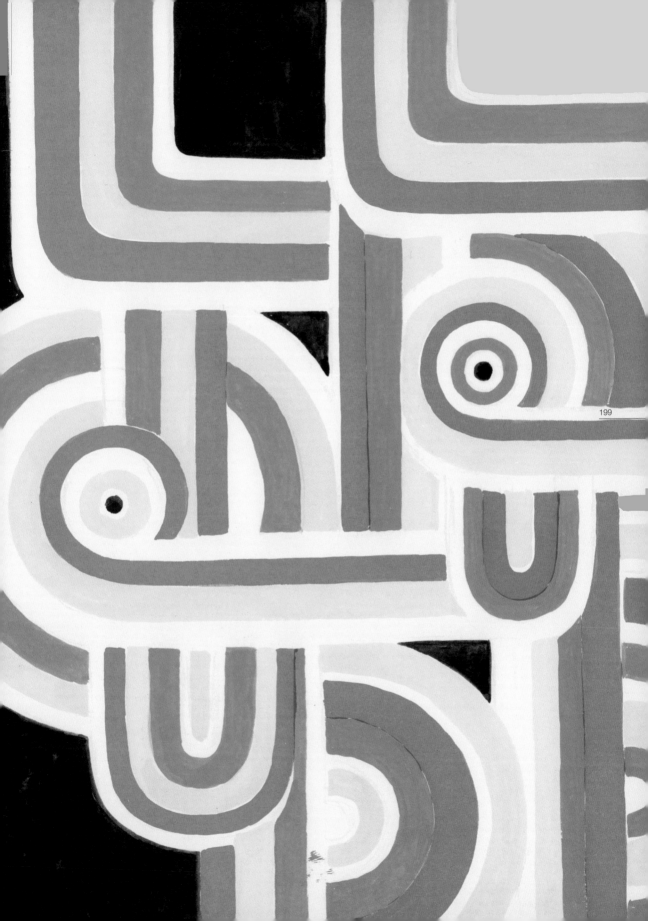

Bernard Maisner

New Jersey-based Bernard Maisner, master hand-letterer and calligrapher, has made a career doing fine penmanship for weddings, films, corporate logos, and advertisements. As a sketcher he works on a project-by-project basis.

"Sometimes ideas are literally sketched out, pencil on paper, and then later I will go in with inking," Maisner explains. "If I am not sure what the client wants, I will make dozens of inked versions using various tools to create to the lettering. One of these designs, or sketches, may be just perfect as final art. More commonly, however, one or more of the words are used as reference points for how to proceed to the next round of development."

However, "Sketching for lettering is not the same as when I sketch as an artist attempting to create artwork. As an artist, I keep a traditional sketchbook, which is really just an organized place to have ideas located in a chronological order."

There is a third form of sketching, which, Maisner explains, "is needed at times for my lettering assignments, when I need to 'construct' letterforms, as opposed to 'writing' letterforms. These letters must be carefully drawn and redrawn to achieve the final shapes desired. Inking takes place after the shapes are approved."

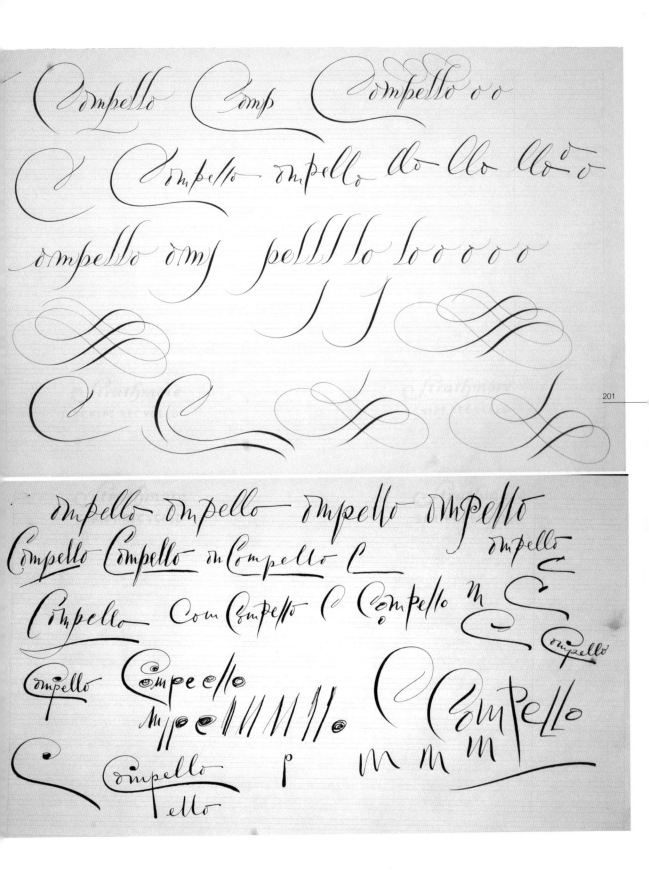

The year was 1929. Herbert Hoover took office and the world was thrown into the despair of the Great Depression. In the midst of worldwide economic calamity, the German & two immigrants founded a small mill in Bally, PA to manufacture men's hosiery. In tribute to their new home and the dream therein, they named it Great American Knitting Mills. In such trying times they desired to create socks that would wear better and last longer. The answer was found in a gold reinforcing yarn sewn in the toe. The Gold Toe® brand. For 80 years the Gold Toe® brand has represented a commitment to crafting socks that are uncommonly comfortable, and reliable, resilient. It is a rigorous standard of quality that has come to stand the test of time.

Quando ho Ricevuto la diagnosi di cancro, la mie vita è cambiata. Avevo bisogno di essere FORTE e ho avuto bisogno di essere FORTE ancora piu FORTE per le mie ossa, e ho avuto bisogno di essere con tutta la mia forza. Questa malattia. Il mio spirito rimane intatto. O giusto bisogno di aiuto. Per continuare ad andare avanti. Poi il cancro ha attaccato le mie ossa, continuerò a combattere.

Javier Mariscal

Barcelona "institution" Javier Mariscal, master of interior, exterior, and graphic design, comics, cartoons, characters, and letterforms, seems to be perpetually drawing. He has even published a hefty book of his sketches, which he's produced since the age of eighteen. "I've been doing sketches of what is natural, of what is around me," says Mariscal. "For me, it's the only way to understand reality because I have many learning problems, probably because I'm dyslexic without ever having been diagnosed. If I want to know what a coffee machine is and how it works, I first have to draw it."

Although his work is often sketchy, sometimes the sketch is very different from his final work. Then again, sometimes they are identical. "I've just done a calendar for the Canadian magazine *Azure* which consists of twelve sketches that I did in Cuba and they were published just as they were. I didn't do them for any particular reason, but later it occurred to me that they could be used for this commission. When I draw, depending on the moment, I can do something highly schematic, or something very elaborate, or I can home in on a small detail."

NIKE
CIUDAD
DE MEXICO

NIKE
TOK
CIUDAD DE
MEXICO
8.3.9

Mm

SUPER.

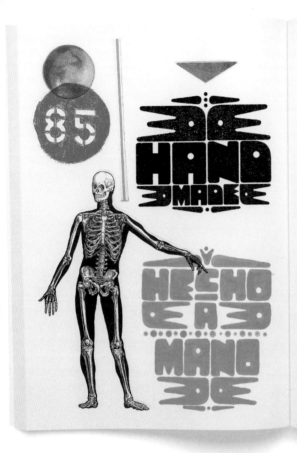

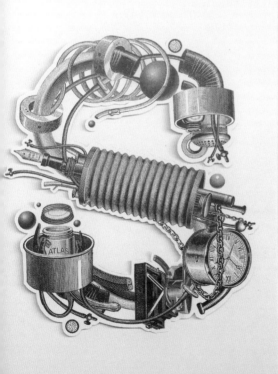

MASA

MASA is the founder of MASA Design in Caracas, Venezuela. His work draws inspiration from his research into Latin American pop and international street culture. He blends urban and folklore references into a contemporary brew for sneaker, streetwear, and snowboard companies.

He notes that "as a picture, a sketch captures the moment, an idea that documents my daily thoughts and my current methodology before it fades like a dream in the morning after." Yet drawings have a grander purpose. "I like to say that now I work as if the finals are just the best sketches with a light evolution. No matter what will be outputted in the end, it's true to my vision."

"The important thing is to achieve a bold result with strength and attitude," he adds. "The same power in a sketch as in the final. No matter what, I never want to repeat a single sketch. It keeps the real...and comes with new discoveries and mistakes along the way. And that's unique." The sketches represent what he calls "absolute improvisation." These images are from 2009 to 2010.

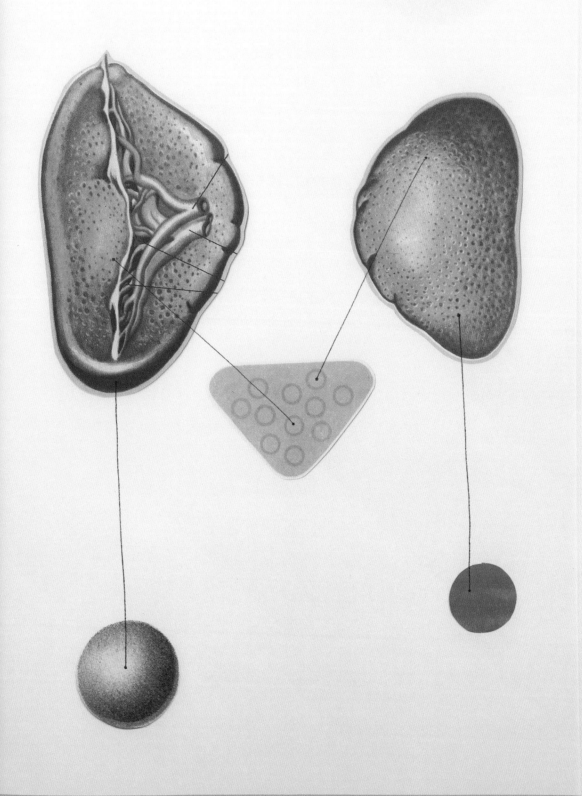

Victor Melamed

Victor Melamed is an illustrator, letterer, and caricaturist living in Moscow. As a tutor, he says, "I insist that each week my students 'spoil' a pile of paper as thick as a finger – and I try to live up to that standard myself."

He mostly sketches from life because "it lets me keep up sharpness of perception and learn more about people's physique, faces, and characters." Depending on the time available he can sometimes use a full sketchbook for one illustration, testing the characters, the story, the details. "But most often I do it entirely in Photoshop. As a matter of fact I regard it as my big problem: the Wacom tablet allows me to produce polished illustrations, portraits especially, but not to preserve the swift quality of the line I enjoy so much in my sketches. I spend hours, days, refining the shapes but then it turns out my first and loosest sketch was more apt than my final work. I'm searching for a new process that would let me blend the two somehow."

His letterforms have a comic quality that expresses the themes he is working with, many of them cultural. Included here is an EP cover and lettering for the band members' names.

PAUL TRACHENKO

GUY SCHLOM

Lemez LoVaS

BEN MANDELSON

Lemez LoVaS

Lemez LoVaS

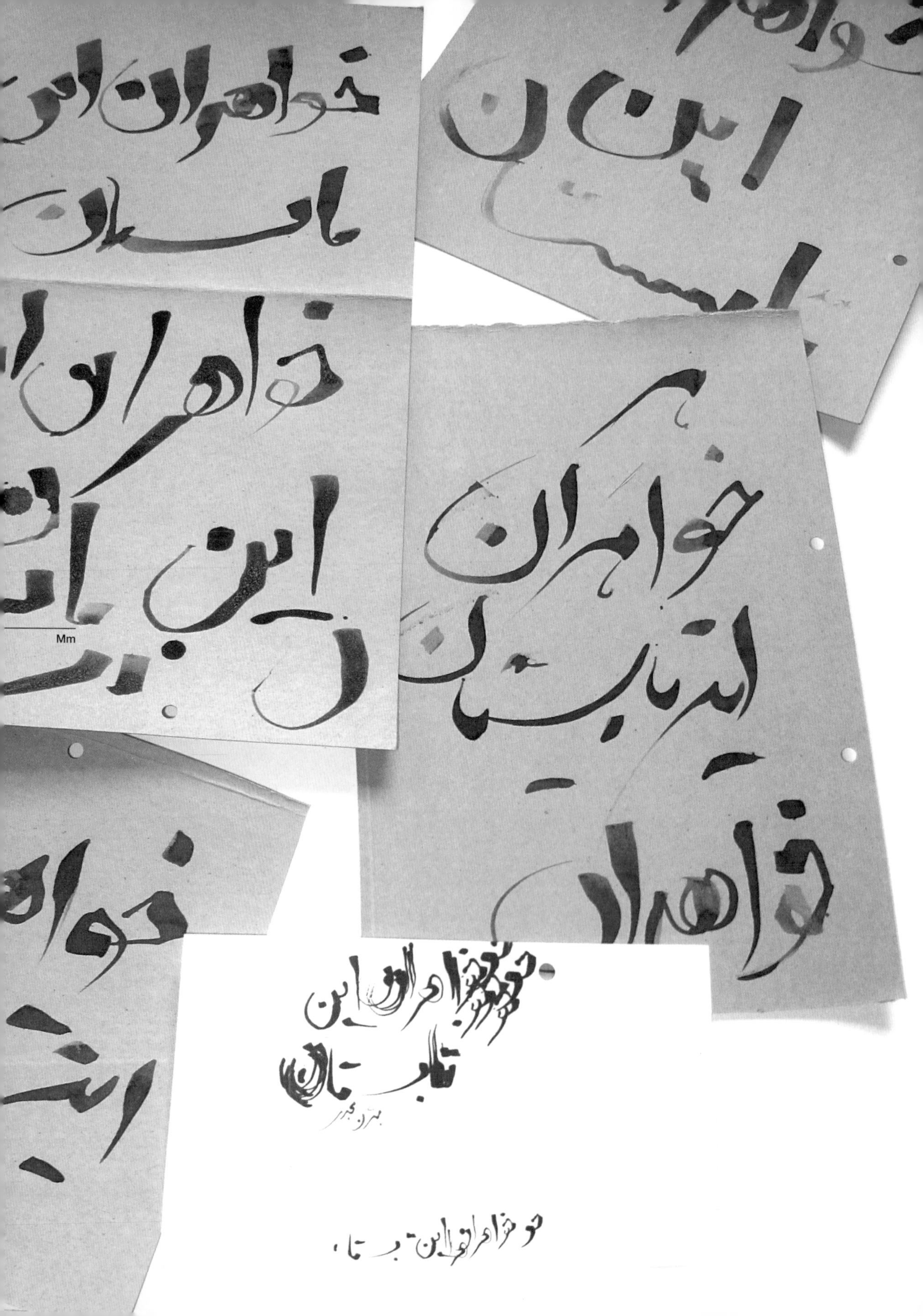

Saed Meshki

Tehran, Iran-based designer Saed Meshki
is known for his wide range of typographic
logo, poster, and book work. He uses
his sketches to "reach the atmosphere
of the subject for which I am sketching,"
he poetically notes. "In fact, I am familiar
with Persian calligraphy. Although my
sketches are not calligraphy, they do have
a calligraphy origin."

Although he designs type, he denies he
is a typographer. "My intention is to use type
as an crucial element to create the image
(illustration) and atmosphere that I would
like to design. In other words, designing
an abstract image with elements that are
readable and comprehensive is my main
concern. This is a difficult combination and
takes time."

Meshki's sketches are the thoughts that
evolve into design. "First I scan these hand-
writings," he explains. "Then I put them next
to each other, add or remove some, and in
some cases I even add textures and repeat
this process till I achieve the design that I am
satisfied with." He adds that these sketches
are done freely, "and indicate a very light
atmosphere, done by a fluid mind."

GOD IS AN IMAGINARY FRIEND FOR GROWN UPS

Niels Shoe Meulman

Niels Shoe Meulman is a graffiti writer and graphic designer from Amsterdam with a special bent for street art. "In my early graffiti years it was the norm to always carry a black book," he notes. "Later, when I ran my design company Caulfield & Tensing in the 1990s, I began scribbling in a book again. I wrote 'Notes 1' on the cover. I'm currently starting a new book, 'Notes 47.'"

For Meulman there are different types of sketch: typographic outlines for logos, and type designs. "I keep forms organic by first sketching by hand before digitizing as vector art," he says. Then there are the more conceptual or textual ideas that he has to write down to remember. Recently he has been writing pages and pages in his "Calligraffiti" style. "Doing that just makes me feel good," he adds. "Some of those words might be the starting point for a bigger piece and end up as framed Calligraffiti art." There is no particular theme in the books, but each sketch provides "a look inside my head. You can see the mood I was in at that moment."

WriteAbility

writeability,

WRITEABILITY

Ross Milne

Ross Milne, from Vancouver, earned his Masters in type and media at the Royal Academy of Art, The Hague (KABK), before traveling to San Francisco, working in several boutique design firms, and finally returning to Canada in early 2009. He is currently a contributing designer with Commercial Type and his typeface Foxtrot is planned for release by Typotheque.

Milne says he's never been someone who "just sketches, even though I constantly wish I was." His sketches are almost always a response to a specific project or idea with a fairly defined goal. "Even in my detailed sketches I try to push off decision-making as long as possible. Often, I find it hard to understand how the terminals of the letters will be, or the amount of contrast in the strokes. Often the sketching process acts as a voice showing you what to do next."

While the hand sketches are quite typical, Milne says that "the use of interpolation tools (in my case, I use Erik van Blokland's Superpolator software) to sketch multiple variations of a wordmark or logotype offers a unique way to visualize numerous options that would otherwise take hours to sketch."

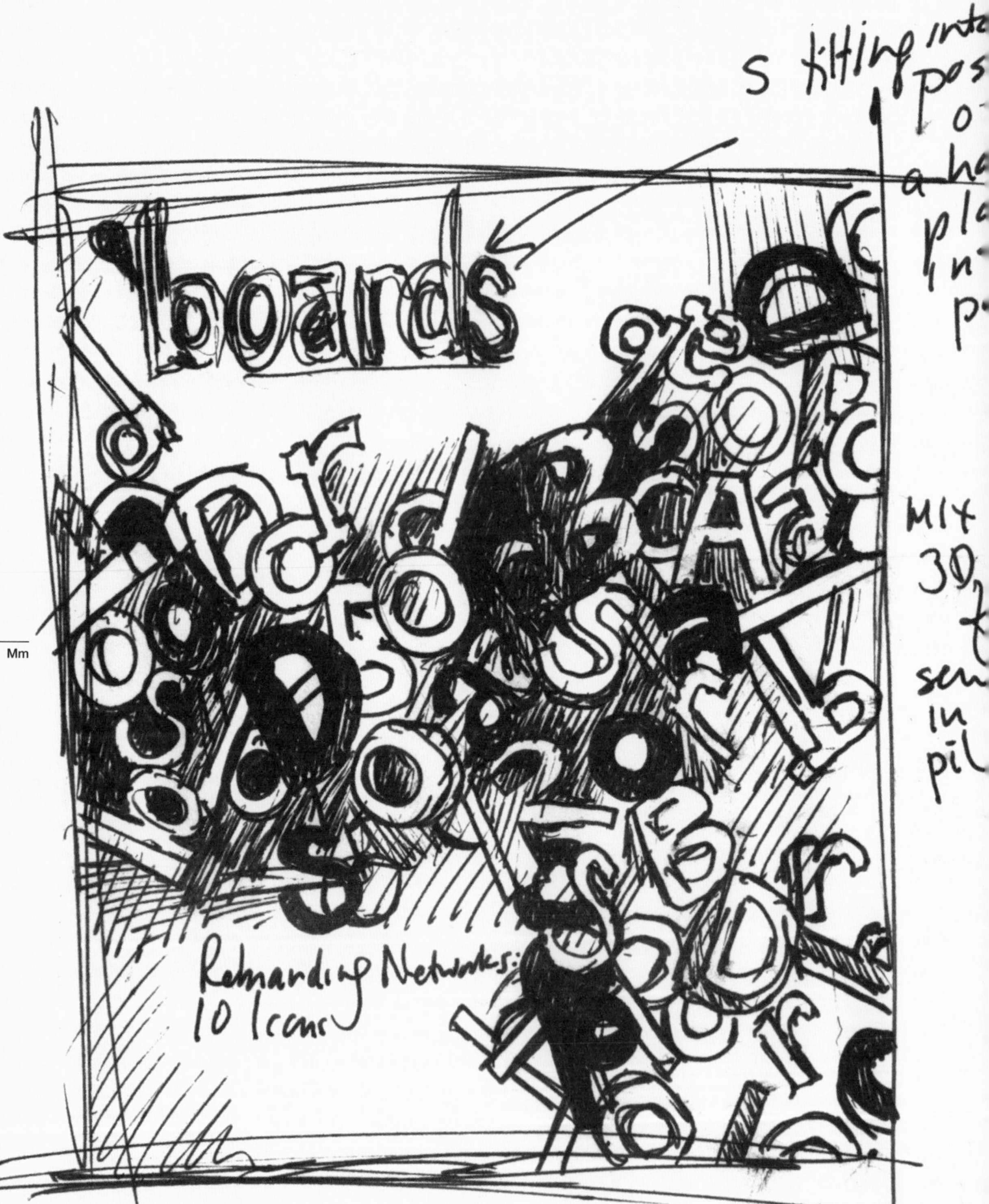

'boards

Rebranding Networks:
10 Icons

s tilting into
pos
o
a ha
pla
in p
p

MIt
30
f
sem
in
pil

Mm

Anna Minkkinen

Anna Minkkinen, Creative Director at Trollbäck + Company in New York, uses sketchbooks for her graphic design work. "My sketches help me to rough out concepts and jot down ideas for all the projects I am working on. Drawing out even very rough storyboards helps me to visualize whether a raw idea will actually work. There are certainly also times where you can't fully express what you want something to feel like stylistically in sketch form – but from a conceptual standpoint it is an important tool. In some ways, the old-fashioned pen on paper keeps me focused on structure and concept and not just on a digital 'look' I might use in the end product."

Minkkinen created these drawings while designing a recent cover of *Boards* magazine, the "design issue" featuring iconic rebrands of the last decade. "I started to imagine this collection of type, all crammed together hodgepodge. I wasn't too sure if the letters would be a mountain or a flurry of flying letters or just a loose pile. Ultimately, it helped me to play with the idea and then to imagine it in sketch form first to see if I had faith in the concept."

طرح اسلیمی پارچه

استدلال کردند اگر کردار های عوامت زندگی که رنگ به رشته طرح صورت فراهد کنند

دو گرگمی دوری به زبان فته کرد

Morteza Momayez

Morteza Momayez (1935–2005) was an Iranian graphic designer and one of the founders of the Iranian Graphic Design Society. He was Editor-in-Chief of *Neshan*, an Iranian graphic design journal, initiated numerous cultural and design initiatives in Iran, and was known for his book jackets and covers.

The sketches here were provided by his colleague and friend, Majid Abbasi, as evidence of his unique skill in creating letterforms. His drawings blend a classical hand and a modern sensibility. The letters and pictures are calligraphic, yet not in the conventional sense – rather, in the fluidity of his line and the expressiveness of his nuance.

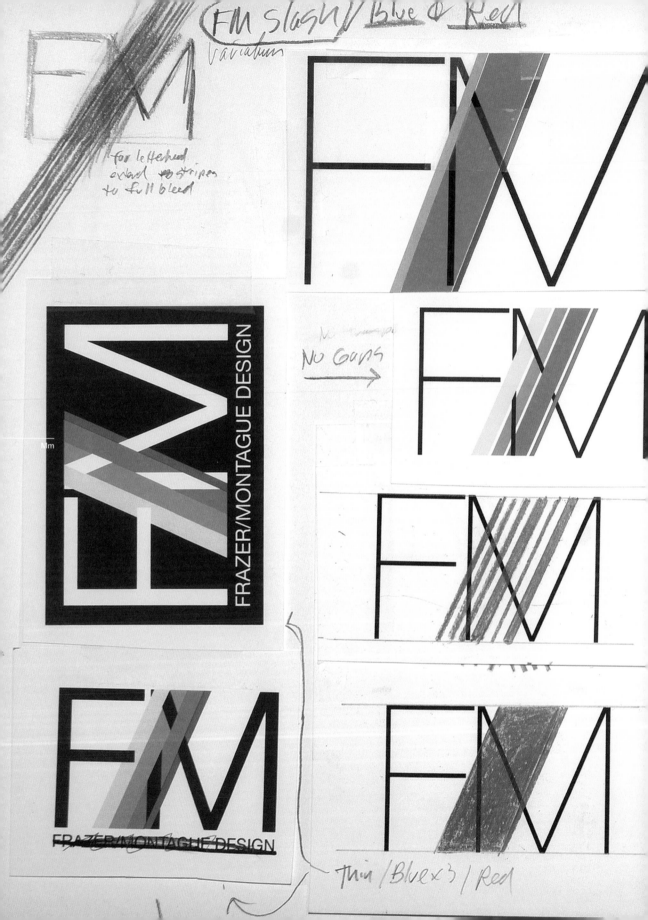

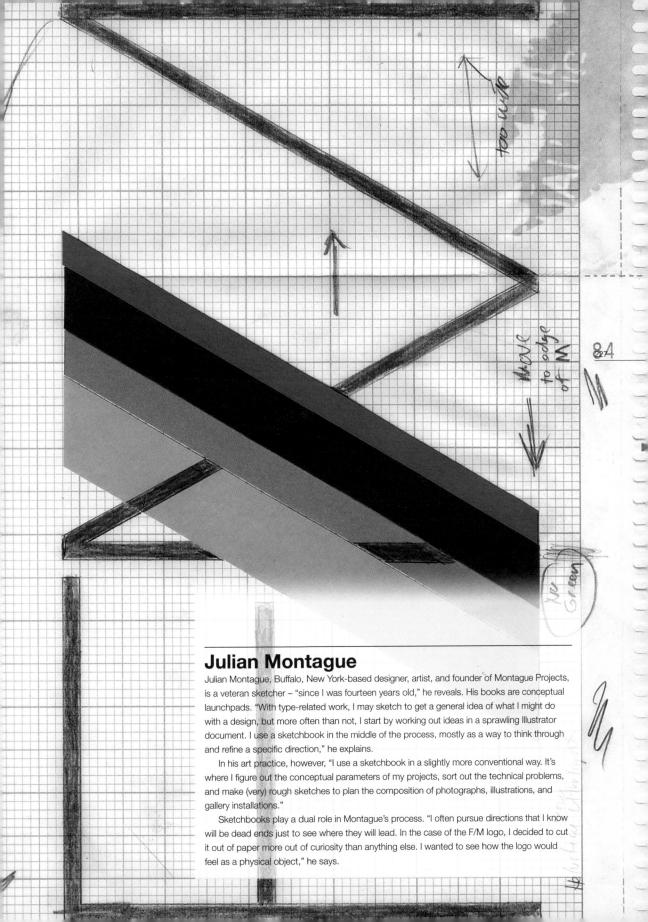

too wide

move
to edge
of W

Julian Montague

Julian Montague, Buffalo, New York-based designer, artist, and founder of Montague Projects, is a veteran sketcher – "since I was fourteen years old," he reveals. His books are conceptual launchpads. "With type-related work, I may sketch to get a general idea of what I might do with a design, but more often than not, I start by working out ideas in a sprawling Illustrator document. I use a sketchbook in the middle of the process, mostly as a way to think through and refine a specific direction," he explains.

In his art practice, however, "I use a sketchbook in a slightly more conventional way. It's where I figure out the conceptual parameters of my projects, sort out the technical problems, and make (very) rough sketches to plan the composition of photographs, illustrations, and gallery installations."

Sketchbooks play a dual role in Montague's process. "I often pursue directions that I know will be dead ends just to see where they will lead. In the case of the F/M logo, I decided to cut it out of paper more out of curiosity than anything else. I wanted to see how the logo would feel as a physical object," he says.

FRAZER/MONTAGUE DESIGN

FRAZER/MONTAGUE DESIGN

FRAZER/
MONTAGUE
DESIGN

FRAZER/
MONTAGUE
DESIGN

FRAZER/
MONTAGUE
DESIGN

FRAZER/MONTAGUE DESIGN

FRAZER/MONTAGUE DESIGN

FRAZER/
MONTAGUE
DESIGN

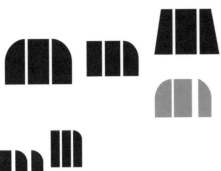

FRAZER/MONTAGUE DESIGN

FRAZER/MONTAGUE DESIGN

FRAZER/MONTAGUE DESIGN

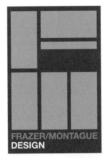

FRAZER/
MONTAGUE
DESIGN

FRAZER/MONTAGUE
DESIGN

FRAZER/
MONTAGUE
DESIGN

FRAZER/
MONTAGUE
DESIGN

FRAZER/MONTAGUE DESIGN

FRAZER/MONTAGUE DESIGN

FRAZER/MONTAGUE DESIGN

FRAZER/
MONTAGUE
DESIGN

FRAZER/
MONTAGUE
DESIGN

FRAZER/
MONTAGUE
DESIGN

FRAZER/MONTAGUE DESIGN

FRAZER/MONTAGUE DESIGN

FRAZER/MONTAGUE DESIGN

FRAZER/
MONTAGUE
DESIGN

FRAZER/
MONTAGUE
DESIGN

James Montalbano

James Montalbano, a New York type designer whose Terminal Design Inc. is responsible for a slew of faces for major American magazines and corporations, including Alfon, Clearview, Consul, Rawlinson, and Trilon, has never actually kept a sketchbook. "I only sketch when I think it will help me solve a problem," he states defiantly. "Early in my career I relied on pencil sketches to develop my ideas. I now draw directly on the computer."

Sketching is neither a casual pastime nor pleasure. "I have no musings; everything I draw has a purpose," he adds. "That purpose may change, but it all starts out as an attempt to solve a problem. They are the beginning of a thought process; the final work is the end of that process."

And yet, sketches abound. "These images are from different times in my career," he relents. "I suppose the most unusual are the Ikarus sketches, which were preparation for a digitizing process I no longer use, but was very important to me early in my career." The Freddo Ikarus sketches (opposite) are from 1995 and the VF Script (this page) from 1999.

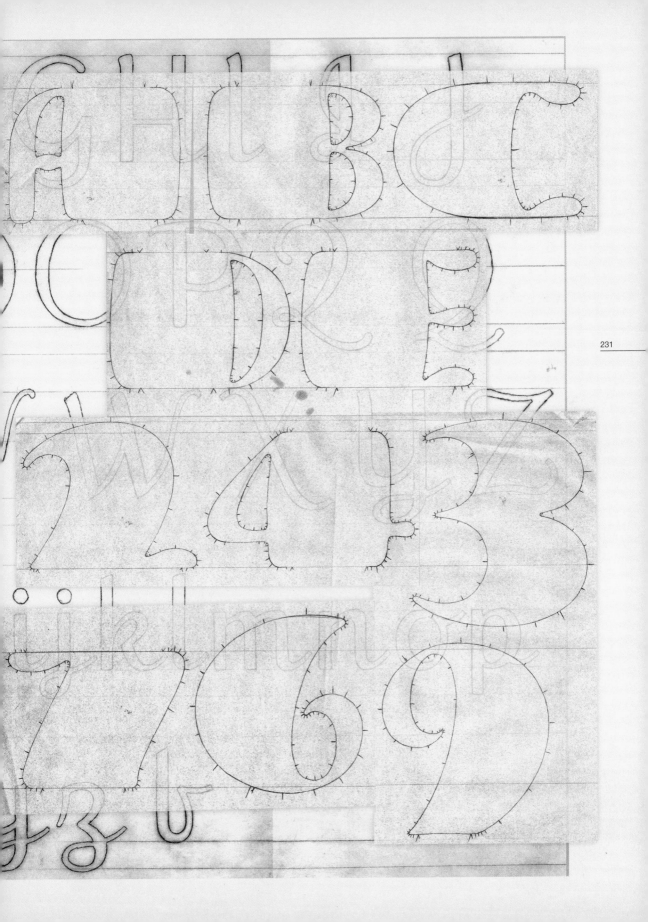

John Moore

John Moore, a type designer in Caracas, Venezuela, uses sketches as "the primary initiative to organize and visualize ideas. I think a good design saves hours of work and allows you to evaluate how creative you can be before moving on to better states of development."

Moore observes that the sketch can have many purposes, "depending on the pressures of work, such as free trial of creative ideas for designing fonts, marks, or signs for a production photo, an illustration, some idea of a 3-D object, an animation sequence, or simply to have fun. In the latter case it becomes a real outlet for any emotional distress."

This outlet enables "a mental state or emotional feeling, a kind of relief of a whole energy concentration." He savors the "spontaneity and looseness of expression" in sketches, which "provides a path that is not achievable by any other means." And, he adds, "the ability to visualize or anticipate in an instant means that difficulty is sometimes overcome by alternatives of expression. Many times the warmth of a sketch may be lost in an elaborate final stage."

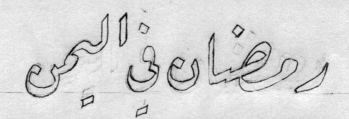

رمضان في اليمن

ramadan in yemen

by

من

Max Pam

Titus Nemeth

Titus Nemeth is an Austrian type designer specializing in Arabic typeface design, typography, and custom type, now living in Paris. He says, "I never trash a sketchbook; I still have my earliest sketchbooks from design school in Vienna."

His current books are venues for working out a detail, or for figuring out a gesture or a movement that he wants to translate into a typographic shape. "I mainly develop ideas on paper, but most of the actual design happens directly on screen. Partly I think that my manual skills are just not up to the task of producing beautiful type shapes, partly it is a question of time: I am simply quicker with Bézier curves than with pencil curves," he explains.

One of the things he admits to enjoying when looking through old sketchbooks are "the random little images, words, notes, thoughts that have ended up on the same pages as some letter shapes that might turn into a commercial typeface. Sketchbooks have something very personal and I must admit I really like some of the little and often weird things I find on some of my pages."

رمضان في اليمن

ramamad.

by

من

Max P

editions bessard paris

nia lion ici allia inclinai
clin clan ailloli al collai
allia al alcalin ai lancina

Characterset: inalco

Language: French

nia lion ici allia inclinai clin clan ailloli al collai

a gloomier seriocomica
acne imam giggling ala
in yemearnalise macaro

Characterset: aesiongrmlc

Language: English

a gloomier seriocomical acne imam giggling ala

hot nudes signala in
amctivaient if gageasses
admiras if attribution

Characterset: acdefghilmnorst.,

Language: German

hot nudes signala invectivaient if gageasses adm
ras if attribution doucirait cul signet moelleuse

LE PAYS BAS OUDT LE P

LE PAYS BA

PANORA

OUDT

LE PAYS BAS OUDT LE P

Niessen & de Vries

Graphic designers Richard Niessen and Esther de Vries are based in Amsterdam – but not just any part of the city. A 2009 article in *Grafik* magazine notes it is in "a beautiful, light-filled live/ work space in Bijlmer in Amsterdam's Zuidoost," a distinctly artistic part of the venerable town.

The couple have worked together under the name Niessen & de Vries since 2007. They originally used the name Typographic Masonry, "creating increasingly bold and adventurous works inspired by architecture, illuminated manuscripts, mosaics, patterns, travelling, Eduardo Paolozzi, Richard Rogers, Ettore Sottsass and many other sources," says Niessen. De Vries worked independently, specializing in artists' books and educational art books for children. Today, she works on her own projects, collaborates with Niessen and also runs Uitgeverij Boek, the small publishing house responsible for their TM-City exhibition catalog.

What about the process of sketching? "I write down my to-do's, and quick ideas," says Niessen. "The real sketches I make on the A4s or A3s that I print out with the first try-outs on the computer. I sketch on the prints, then work on the computer again, make a new printout and sketch again."

TEXT

PANORAMA

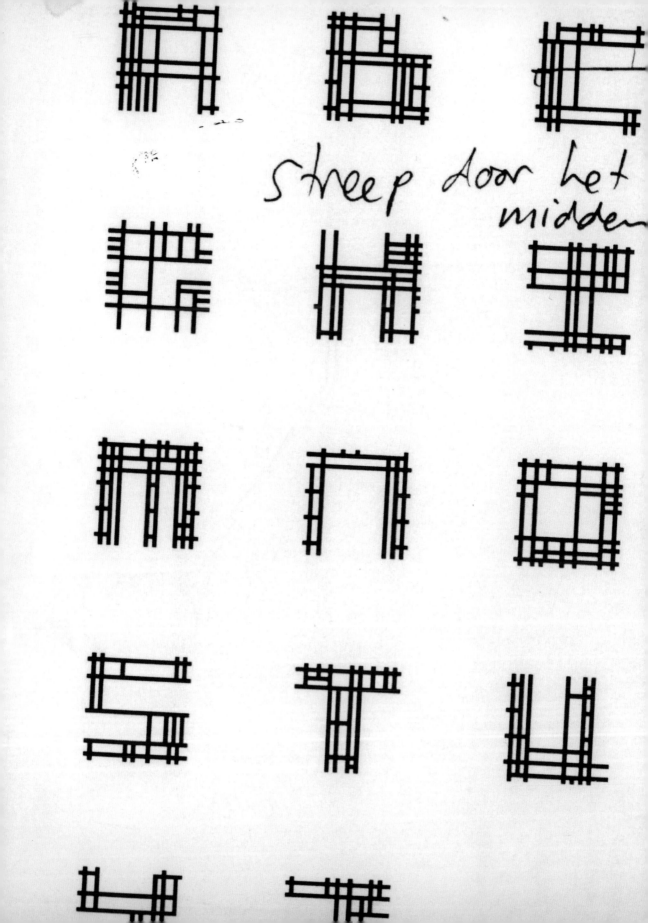

streep door het midden

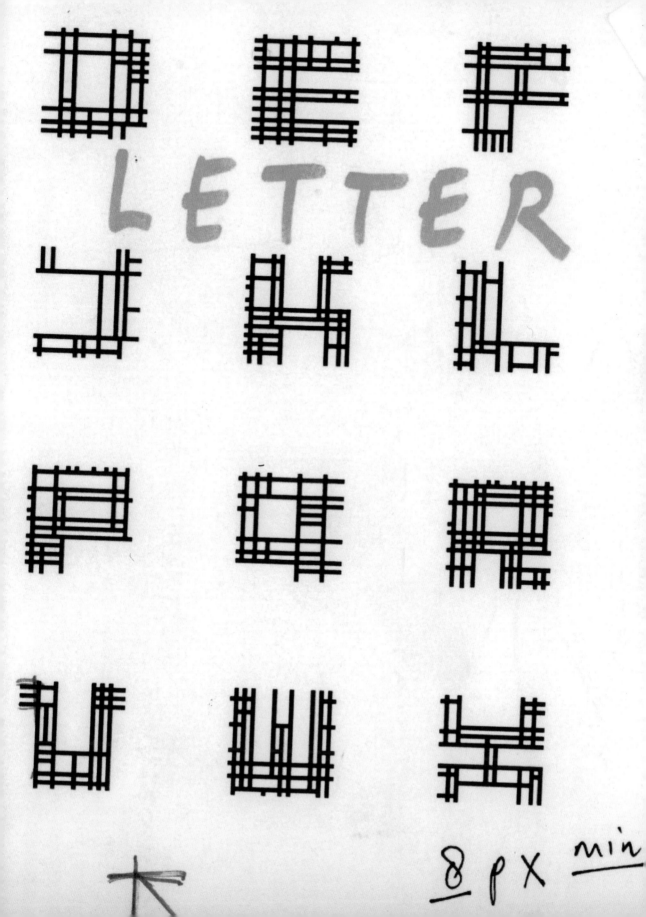

LETTER

8 px min

ABCDEFG H Y
MCJFLNEW YE
ABCDEFGGHJKL
MMMMMMNOPQR

ABCDEFGHJKLM
ANNOPQRST
VWXYZ.,9?!

Nn

1234567890/()+÷×

DARJELING
OPEN MATCH
&X
LWФXZ

PATTER KOMO

Futura Black

OMBRA → Othmar Motter , Allegro → Hans Bohn   www.neufville.com   Hanta   VN-DSGN.DE

Viktor Nübel

Viktor Nübel is a graphic and typographic designer in Berlin, who designed the typeface PTL Attack and works with FontShop International. All his faces have a decorative component, notably Ostblock, a typeface made of three-dimensional forms. Nübel's experimental types include Modul72, a totally abstract selection of glyphs that take the form of letters, and Type Attack! (overleaf), which is the stencil version of Attack and comes as a sheet of shapes that can be spray-painted on any surface. "The Attack typeface was my thesis in design school," Nübel states. "I wanted to create a 'corporate' typeface for the anti-globalization network. I thought of doing something that can be used in printed material as well as on banners and hand-made posters. So I came up with the idea of a stencil, a stencil every activist can use and that is small enough to carry."

For the Oliva typeface (these pages) Nübel had the idea to combine two typefaces – Futura Black and Motter Ombra, each with a strong display impression. "In the beginning I just had the idea for a few upper-case letters," Nübel states. "So I started to draw the whole alphabet and soon recognized that it was not easy on some letters to find the right shape. It really took a while."

→ darans nochmal
einen font machen!

TSKYXV→ Problemfälle

BASIC SET

ATC NotForSale™ Schablone

Sketch Size

ATTAC BANNER · SIZE 120PT.

← Buchstabenabstand war!

ATTAC METAL

NOT FOR SALE!

ATC NotForSale™ Schablone

Sketch Size

ATTAC FRAKTUR

Å B Ç Ď É F G

H I J K L M

Ñ Ö P Q R S T

Ü V W X Y Z

1 2 3 4 5 6 7

8 9 0 . , ! ?

ABCCCDDDEF
GHIJKLMNOP
QRSTUVWXYZ
IIIIIIIIIIIIIIPIIRS
PPRUVBCCDE
IABCCDEFGGG
GHHIJEEEEFE
TUVWXXXY

ABCDEFGHIJK
LMNOPQRSTU
VWXYZ ABC
DEFGHIJKLMN
OPQRSTUVWX
YYZUUUUUUU
FLUKE&
FRIENDS

Gary Panter

Gary Panter, the Texas-raised, Brooklyn-based comics artist and creator of the Punk anti-hero "Jimbo," is known for a burlesque of various different themes and forms. He is a hoarder of thoughts, images and more thoughts. "In sketchbooks I throw every idea in," Panter crows. "Some of them will be developed further, some are scribbles and warm-ups and wrong moves. The activity, in general, is hopeful and ambitious."

His books are like his Brooklyn studio: chaotic yet brimming with incredible stuff, especially lettering, which goes through a wealth of permutations. "Sketchbooks are about getting a flow of ideas going," he adds. "Letting the good, bad, and indifferent out. Then I start to rearrange or play with the fragments and see if they will build into something else." His finished art is most often more refined, "or bigger, or in color, or sculptural, or something that takes it out of the book, but not too far from the initial context."

When asked what purpose the sketches have in his life, he cryptically and cosmically notes, "I am trying to remember the future with them. There are various themes and obsessions that come back: robotics, architecture, dinosaurs, monsters, human figure drawing, cartoon characters, signs, painting notes, music notes, and all have resonance as letterforms."

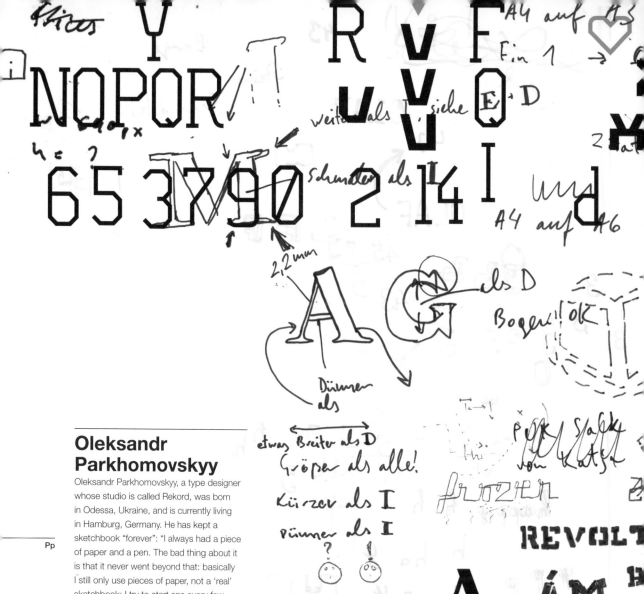

Oleksandr Parkhomovskyy

Oleksandr Parkhomovskyy, a type designer whose studio is called Rekord, was born in Odessa, Ukraine, and is currently living in Hamburg, Germany. He has kept a sketchbook "forever": "I always had a piece of paper and a pen. The bad thing about it is that it never went beyond that: basically I still only use pieces of paper, not a 'real' sketchbook; I try to start one every few months, but it never goes beyond a few pages. Sooner or later (mostly sooner) I find myself sketching on another piece of paper, which becomes the current to-do list, and thus too valuable to throw away."

Parkhomovskyy claims he almost never sketches out of boredom or while talking on the phone. No doodling for him. "I don't make refined sketches though – all the next steps happen digitally. I rely on my memory, that it will catch the hint I thought of while sketching. I take the rough visual notes to look at the concept in a much faster way than using a computer," he says.

These sketches are from 2008 to 2010. But, he admits, "I have a habit of drawing current information on very old sketches, another trait of my imperfect organization. So it's hard to tell."

Stencil

Regular WHITE

Rounded

Black

Rounded

visit sites to read

Votings

Best Logos
Font of the day
Software
Amazon
Free Fonts

Umbrella!

Pizza Dude

Flat it

Fontfarm

Add Icons to Post Titles

Auto

AN

RG

RE

ER

HELLO

Icons?

ABCDE

ABCD→EF

6789 123456<8

CORMAC McCARTHY

THE ROAD

A WORK OF SUCH TERRIBLE BEAUTY THAT YOU WILL STRUGGLE TO LOOK AWAY

THE TIMES

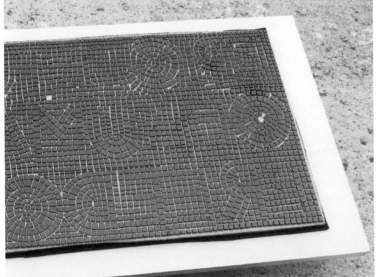

David Pearson

A typographic designer based in Clerkenwell, London, who specializes in book design and branding, David Pearson has either designed or commissioned some of the most illustratively and typographically unique books on today's shelves. His covers for Penguin are at once playful and reflective of printing history.

"I have never been a great draftsman," he says of his sketches, "but I am increasingly taking the development stage away from the computer in an attempt to produce work with more character. Cheap, homogenized printing is commonplace in trade publishing, and what appears to be an annual downgrading of materials means that we have to be ever more resourceful in producing tactile and engaging designs."

Pearson happily admits, "It is no secret that many of my heroes worked in a different age, and as an avid collector of their work I am reminded that modern-day book production yields an entirely different physical object. The sole aim of contemporary printing seems to be to eradicate imperfections or any trace of a book's construction, and it is exactly these things (ink squash, variable impression, subtle mis-registration) that delight and engage my senses. So, essentially, I am trying to build a level of unpredictability into the book's conception."

Daniel Pelavin

New York-based illustrator, letterer, and type designer Daniel Pelavin answers an abrupt, no-nonsense "Always!" to the question: How long have you kept a sketchbook? He is the designer of such retro faces as the Deco-style Anna and Bokar Moderne, and Art Nouveau Bing and Rilke, among others. His lettering art is bold, historical, and ornate.

He says he is in his fourth decade of "transforming and melding the images and cultural ephemera of our times into cogent and compelling messages for publishing, advertising, and communication design." A lifelong fascination with dimensional forms has taken him beyond the realm of the graphic page into the world of three-dimensional modeling and rendering; he aspires to create not merely images but objects, products, and devices whose usefulness is enhanced and extended by the eloquence of their design and construction. "Joy," he notes, with a sheepish grin, "is derived from drawing masterfully complex compositions." And sketches "are routinely produced for the pure pleasure of drawing and imagining, and as concepts for solving illustration or design problems."

Pelavin's favorite sketchbook themes are rocket ships, automobiles, consumer appliances, lighthouses, fountain pens, and mechanical contraptions, but type is up there too. The drawings shown here were produced between 1980 and 2010.

Ŧ Ŧ μ ~ ◇

Daniel Pelavin

Berlin Germany California

Elevator Fantasy Hindenberg

Israel Jump Kelp

Land Moonbeam 1234

Number Ornamental 4

Pudzwalker Quigley 5(

Rumplestiltskin Salivary 6

Thurston United 7

Daniel a a c a 9

a a a a D A 10

A D 7 G e 0

Pel

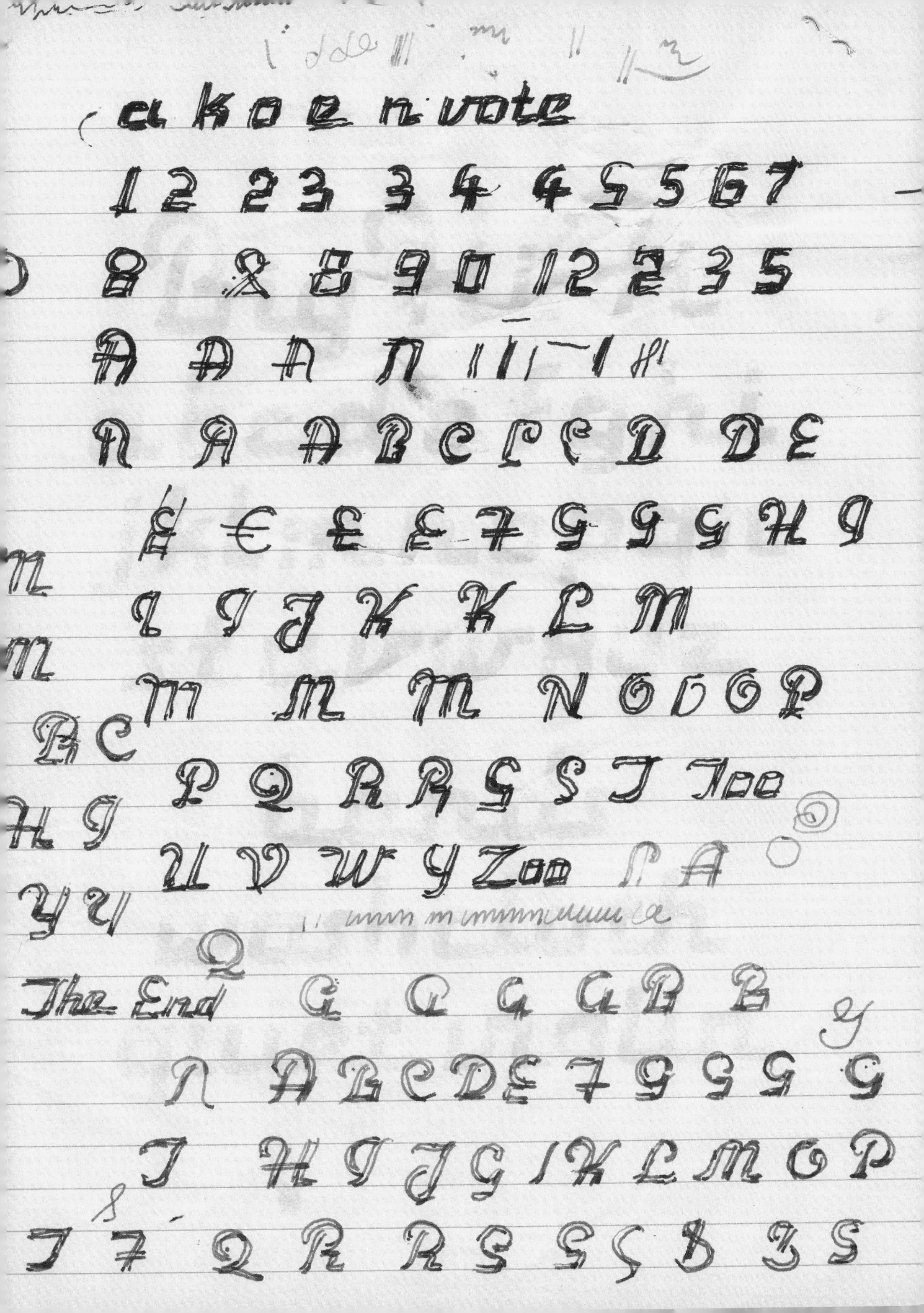

a k o e n vote

1 2 2 3 3 4 4 5 5 6 7

8 8 8 9 0 1 2 2 3 5

A A A A N III ~1 H

N R A A B C C D E D E

H € € £ 7 G G G H I

l I J K K L M

m M M N O O P

B C

P Q R R S S T Too

H I

U V W Y Zoo P A

u m m m m a

The End G C G G B B

N A B C D 3 7 9 9 9 g

I H I J G K L M O P

7 7 Q R R S S S B 3 S

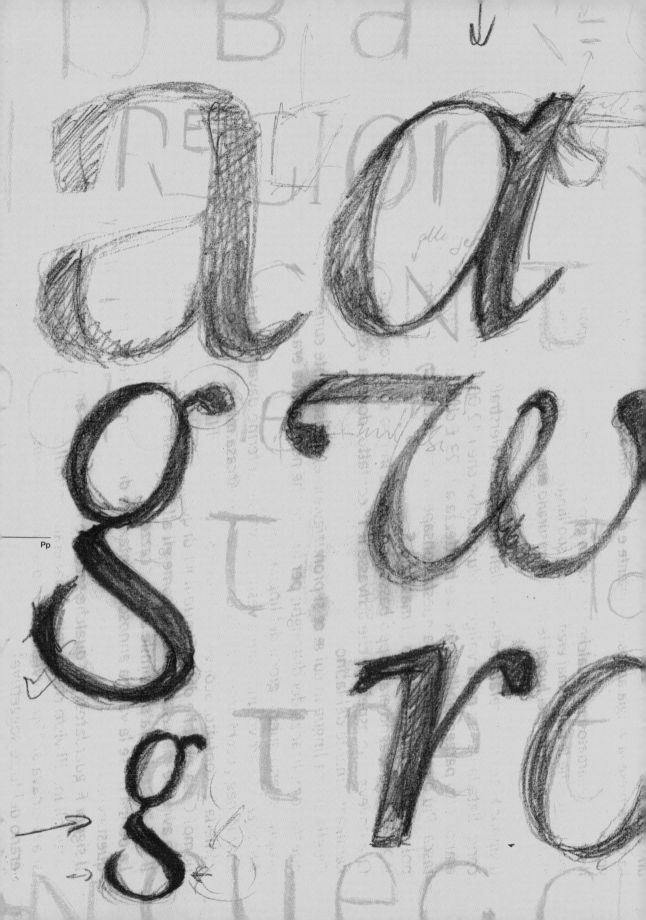

Luciano Perondi

Luciano Perondi is a Milanese typeface, graphic, and information designer. In 2003 he founded Molotro, a studio that creates custom and commercial typefaces and graphic and information design. Interested in writing systems, he has developed several typefaces for corporate identities, events, publishers, and signage systems.

His sketches are not necessarily related to a project that he is working on. "I use sketches to explain something to somebody (or at least this should be the purpose), or to explain something to me (i.e. to think, or at least to pretend to). A couple of years ago my students said that, when I'm lecturing, I always draw some sketches with my finger on my hand, but I never realized that, until they told me," he says.

Perondi fatalistically states, "I should admit my sketches are almost useless for me, but I think that there is a relation between drawing and trying to make order in my mind; it constrains me to show if what I'm thinking has a sense, a structure or not. In the same way, an unusual action (for example, drawing letters on a beach) makes me reflect in a different way on expected shapes (after years of type designing, sometimes I fear to use a sort of 'autopilot')."

YOU HAVE BEEN WARNED NO

Sam Piyasena

London-based illustrator, hand-letterer, and designer Sam Piyasena, known professionally as Billie Jean, has always kept a sketchbook of sorts. "When I was a child, I took great pleasure in sticking things into scrapbooks. My present-day sketchbooks carry on this tradition and are a cocktail of sketches, found objects, photographs, quotes, telephone doodles, and the scribbles of my daughter," he says.

"I'm often commissioned to produce hand-drawn lettering," he continues. "The uninhibited mark-making and fluidity in my sketches can be difficult to replicate in a final outcome. These second-generation drawings can sometimes look too manicured. However, thanks to the wonders of digital technology, I can scan the original sketches and use them in the final piece."

Piyasena's sketchbooks, including the ones here from 2008 to 2010, are usually "a private affair, and so it's incredibly unusual for me to show them to anyone! The 'YOU HAVE BEEN WARNED' image is a sketch for a headline in the *Ecologist* magazine. The others are self-initiated sketches."

BREAKFAST
LUNCHEON
SUPPER
BREAKFAST
LUNCH
DINNER
BREAKFAST
DINNER
TEA

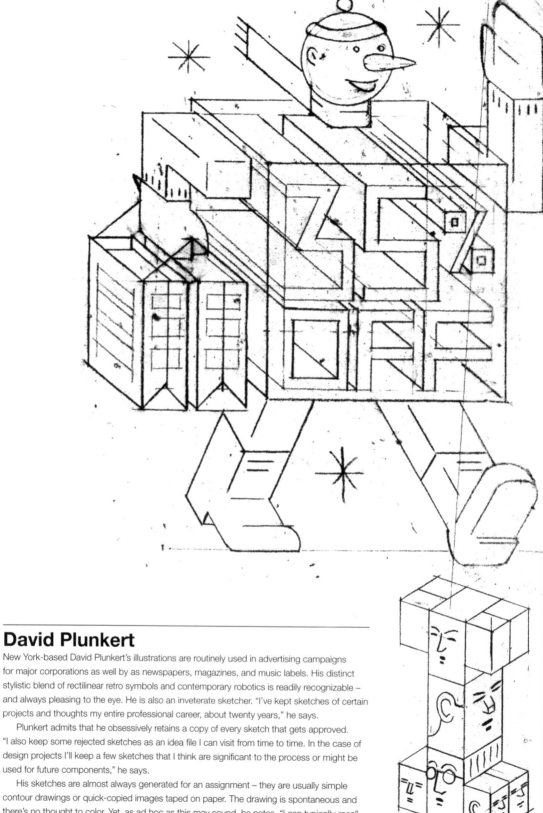

David Plunkert

New York-based David Plunkert's illustrations are routinely used in advertising campaigns for major corporations as well by as newspapers, magazines, and music labels. His distinct stylistic blend of rectilinear retro symbols and contemporary robotics is readily recognizable – and always pleasing to the eye. He is also an inveterate sketcher. "I've kept sketches of certain projects and thoughts my entire professional career, about twenty years," he says.

Plunkert admits that he obsessively retains a copy of every sketch that gets approved. "I also keep some rejected sketches as an idea file I can visit from time to time. In the case of design projects I'll keep a few sketches that I think are significant to the process or might be used for future components," he says.

His sketches are almost always generated for an assignment – they are usually simple contour drawings or quick-copied images taped on paper. The drawing is spontaneous and there's no thought to color. Yet, as ad hoc as this may sound, he notes, "I can typically recall when I've drawn a sketch, whereas creating final art tends to be less memorable."

NUDe

RICHard THOMPSON

Bondé Prang

Bondé Prang, from Wilmington, Delaware, has kept a journal since high school. And while her journal is more for personal things, she maintains scores of boxes full of sketches that were done on tracing paper.

Her sketches usually start as roughs. "Then, I begin to tighten up that sketch by tracing it over and over again," she says. "Each time it becomes tighter and more refined. I do this until I reach something that I am satisfied with, and that will not need too many adjustments once it is scanned into the machine."

Drawing is a healthy break from the computer, "since I rely so heavily on it on a daily basis. I also like to sketch and draw because it shows through in the finished, digitized piece – there are organic curves in a hand-drawn bit of lettering that would not translate as well if I started drawing with the pen tool with no sketch to use as a template."

Most of Prang's typefaces are based on late 1960s and early 1970s-era psychedelic lettering and amateur sign painting. "I'm a fan of pop culture from that time period and those styles of letterforms are quite appealing to me, so it often shows up in my work," she says.

Purgatory
Pie Press

Purgatory Pie Press, a letterpress and print publisher in New York, is named after a moment in 1977 when co-founder Dikko Faust "pied" (or dropped and smashed) a case full of eight-point Century Old Style. In 1980 Faust married Esther K. Smith; their wedding invitation was their first letterpress collaboration.

Smith has dutifully kept sketchbooks on and off since college. "My drawing professor had us draw for something like six hours per week, so it became a habit. And now I sketch for different reasons – sometimes just to draw, sort of for fun, sort of as an exercise – maybe the way knitters knit? Other times to work out an idea, or make notes of ideas as they come up – the way I keep a notebook for writing."

The examples here are typographic sketches "that are different from what I do in average sketchbooks. They are part of our collaborative process," she says. "First we talk – and possibly scribble something. Then Dikko sets type and proofs some things, I cut it up and move it around into a rough paste-up and he sets that up on the press and proofs. Then we fine-tune, and eventually, finally, *voilà!*"

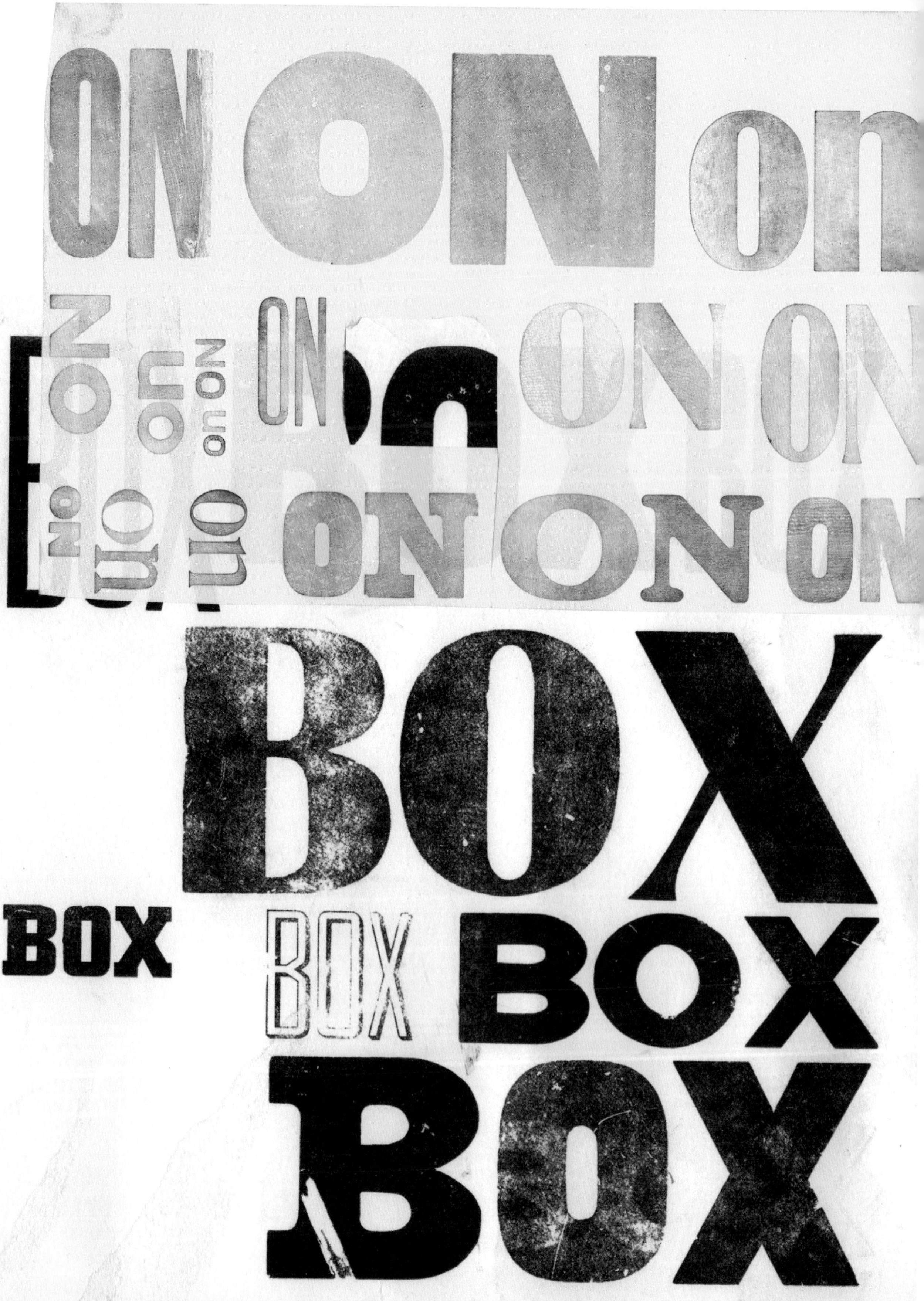

ON ON ON ON on
ON ON ON on on on on on
on on ON ON ON ON
on ON ON ON ON ON

BOX
BOX BOX BOX BOX
BOX

... by Esther K Smith & Dikko Faust set & printed Concave Tuscan & French Clarendon & Afalic & Roman & Gothic &c wood types,   www.PURGATORYPIEPRESS.com

AaBbEeFfGg

HhIiMmNnOo

RrSsUuVvDp

AaBbEeFfGgHhIi

AaBbEeFfGgHhIi

MmNnOoRrSsTt

MmNnOoRrSsTt

UuVvDp UuVvDp

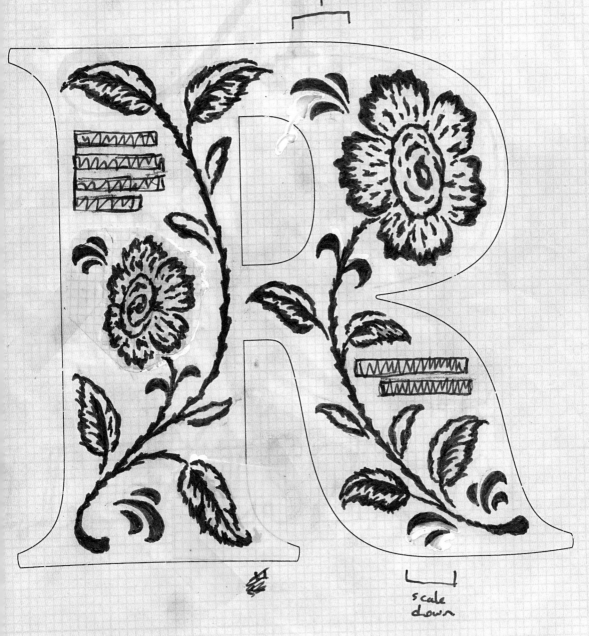

scale
down

Jesse Ragan

Jesse Ragan, a type designer based in Brooklyn, has kept a sketchbook since school days in 1997, but "my diligence fluctuates. Sometimes I go for months without sketching much at all. When I've had longer train/subway commutes in the past, my sketchbook has been far more fertile. It's a productive way to pass the time and escape my surroundings."

Sketching, he admits, keeps his creativity limber: "Designing on a computer encourages efficiency, systematic thinking, and simplification. Drawing letterforms by hand allows the immediacy of a purely visual interface, an organic process in which mathematics and geometry can be ignored more easily. Sketching is Ragan's way to transcend the limitations and tendencies of Bézier curves.

Sketching also comes into play at several points in the development of a project. "After I've drafted a digital prototype version of a design and printed it out, I usually draw more sketches by hand, to brainstorm solutions for the problems I've diagnosed in my printouts. Approaching problems from a different angle often helps me get unstuck," he explains. The proof of Cedar Italic (opposite, bottom) was a turning point, "when I figured out what why the structure of the italic wasn't working in relation to the roman."

Rr

RED

Sam Eckersley and Stuart Rogers, Brooklyn-based founders of RED (Rogers Eckersley Design) speak with one voice when it comes to their sketching. Recalling when they started keeping sketchbooks, they chime: "If a math notebook with not a lot of math and a lot of doodles counts, then we started in grammar school."

The math-book abandon may be gone, but the joy of sketching remains. "Usually, sketches are intended to solve a specific design problem given by a client. Other times, they don't have an immediate purpose. Like our alphabets, we do them because they're fun and could possibly have some future use. We don't think there is one right way to sketch. A sketch is about getting to the core idea quickly, so it could be pencil, fabric, metal, cut paper, or whatever else gets the job done."

RED's sketches are less deliberate than the finished product. There is always an abundance of hand-made letters, and often references to baseball and beer.

"Usually, sketches like these don't see the light of day, so we're not making them for an audience to evaluate. They end up looser, and sometimes – if we're honest about it – more interesting than the finished work."

These images were made between 2007 and 2009.

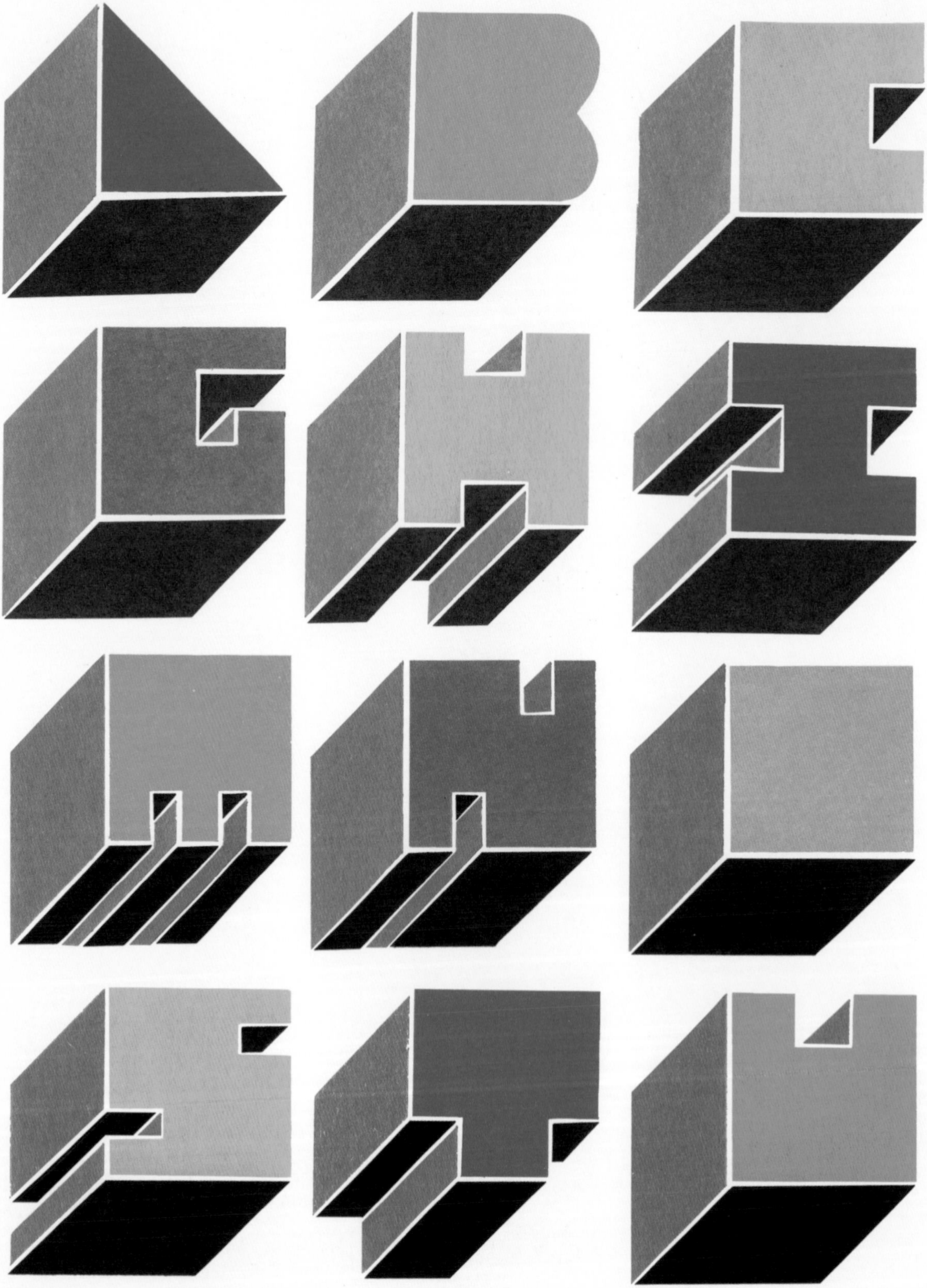

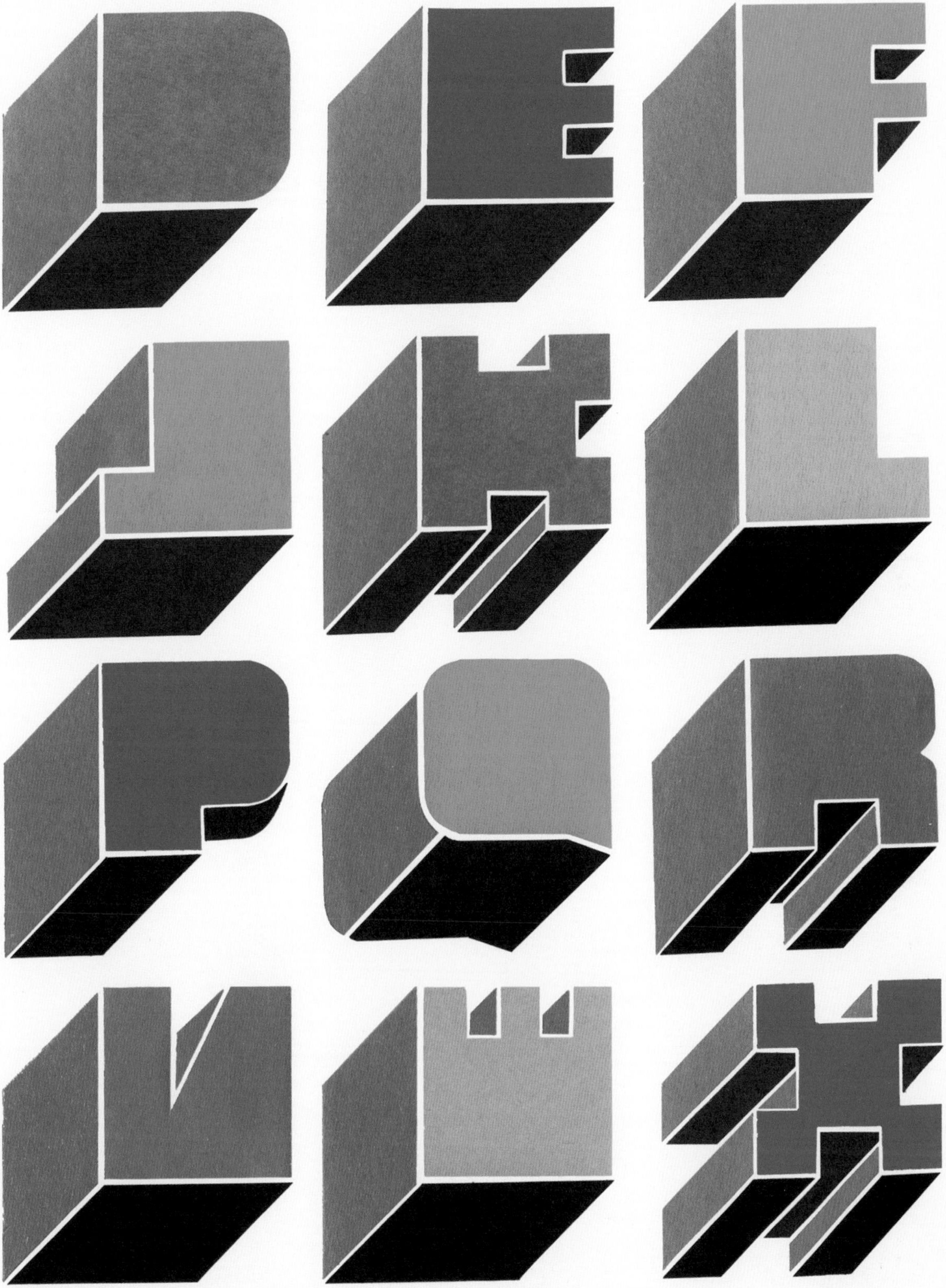
D E F
J K L
P Q R
V W X

PRATA
C/PRETO

Claudio Rocha

Brazilian type designer (ITC Gema, ITC
Underscript and Persplexitiva), publisher of
the type journal *Tupigrafia*, and letterpress
maven Claudio Rocha has been hoarding
sketches since he established his São
Paulo print shop in 2003. Usually these
sketches are part of the production process
in any given letterpress project. In fact,
"most of them were produced to guide the
typesetting and were kept to explain to
students how a project evolves from the idea
to the final print," explains Rocha.

The sketches are preliminary studies, he
says, "but sometimes the layout changes
during the work at the composing room,
when we face the materiality of the types.
The proofs, with detailed instructions,
serve as a record of the process but have
a particular flavor. Maybe they could be
considered a kind of finished work."

Technically, proofs and discarded
sheets are not sketches – but they are, in
a sense, industrial-age sketches that "show
textures and colors that don't belong to the
finished work."

Rr

Zyxwv U

IDEM   ↑ NÃO   IDEM   IDEM   IDEM

tsRQPO

275

IDEM   IDEM   IDEM   IDEM   IDEM

nmLKJ

NÃO ↑

ihGfed

↑ NÃO   IDEM   IDEM   IDEM

cBa.

...eeeïïï

ãããâhnnnnn.????

HMM

ARE

PALAVRAS.
PALAVRAS
SÃO SÓPOR
PALAVRAS

YOU DON'T HAVE TO.

JACK

THE TEACHING STANCE

Jeff Rogers

Illustrator Jeff Rogers, from Dallas, Texas, and now based in New York, modestly notes, "I think some of these sketches look like something you could find in some high school kid's notebook. But hopefully they're a *little* better."

For Rogers, "sketches are inherently line-driven. I love the quality you get with a good ol' pencil – it feels like it was drawn quickly in the moment, light and airy and fast," he says. "My finished work tends to be colorful and bold, but I always like to add paper texture to it. I love the way a sketch feels on a piece of paper: nice and warm and personal. Special. So I pull that back in with texture. I also love to sketch faces – capturing expressions. With type, it is capturing an expression with line, or drawing letterforms in bad 3-D perspective."

Surprisingly, Rogers has done these sketches only since 2009. "Before that I never sketched type. It was always figurative. I have really fallen in love with hand-drawn type over the past year or two."

He adds, "Over the last few years my sketches have served the purpose of getting design ideas out quickly. But I still love to draw and doodle for fun. It could be type ideas or drawing from interesting photos I find on Flickr, usually of people and faces."

Rr

MOUNTAINS are the BEGINNING AND END of all natural SCENERY

—John Ruskin

MOUNTAIN (PERSON)

the CURE for ANYTHING is SALT WATER

SWEAT, TEARS or the SEA.

—ISAK DINESEN

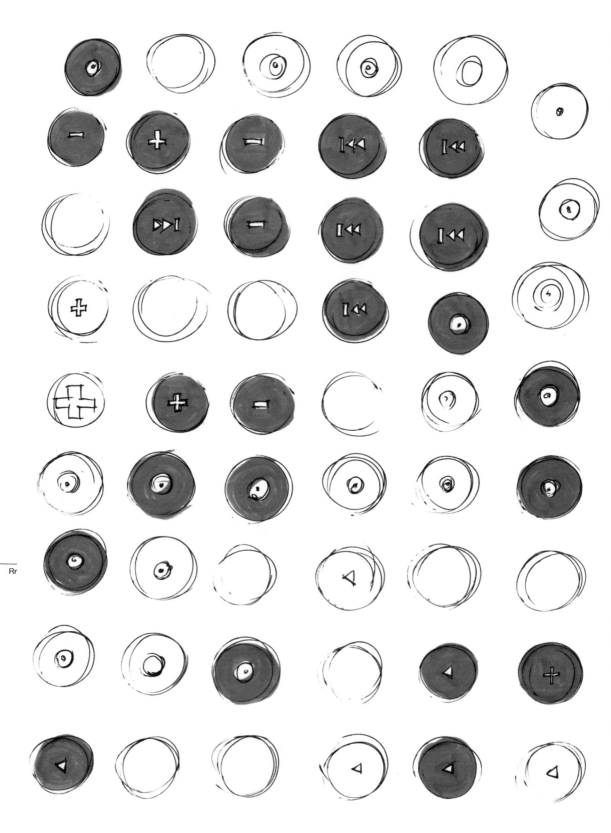

Water ⟶ cold fresh water

   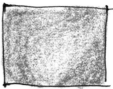

song: A A A A song: E E E E

song: syllable, note
type: character

⟶ vowels are sung + consonants are written.

speech: "W" speech: "T" speech: "R"

⟶ consonants are spoken + vowels are written.

Christina Rüegg

Christina Rüegg, originally from Switzerland, has been Art Director at Trollbäck + Company in New York since 2004. She has kept sketchbooks since about 1996, "but really started using them more intensely in 2004 to manifest ideas, thoughts and concepts."

Rüegg's sketches play a big part in the creative process. "They help me to think and develop ideas," she says. "Some of my sketches are a beginning of a thought, some become more elaborate, some inspire for more thinking, and although they all act as a starting point, few make it into a final piece." Her sketches show the concept and are often a rawer, looser reference or idea for the composition and story, which becomes more refined in the finished piece. The sketches excerpted here were all for Trollbäck projects, 2006–9.

Construction and Zoom

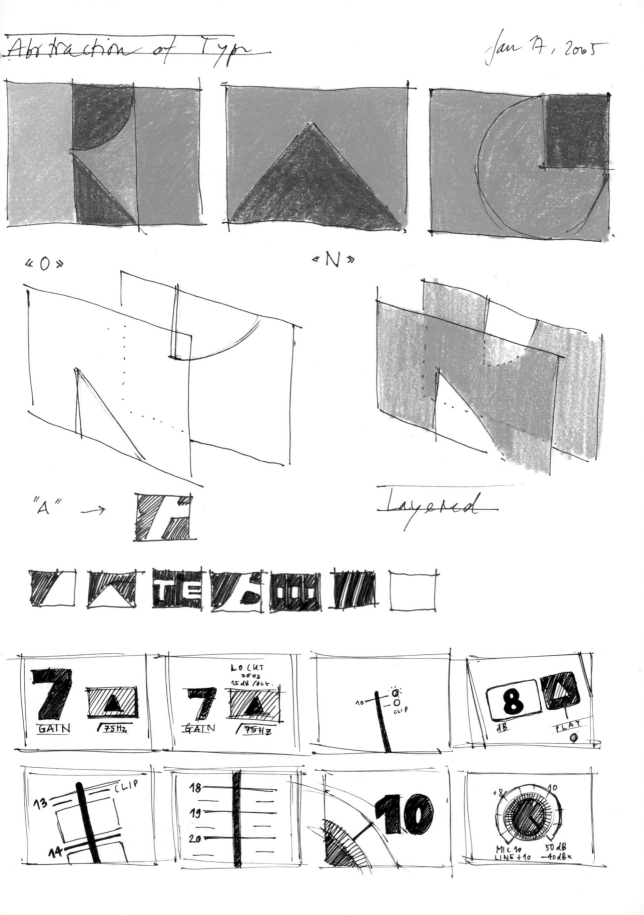

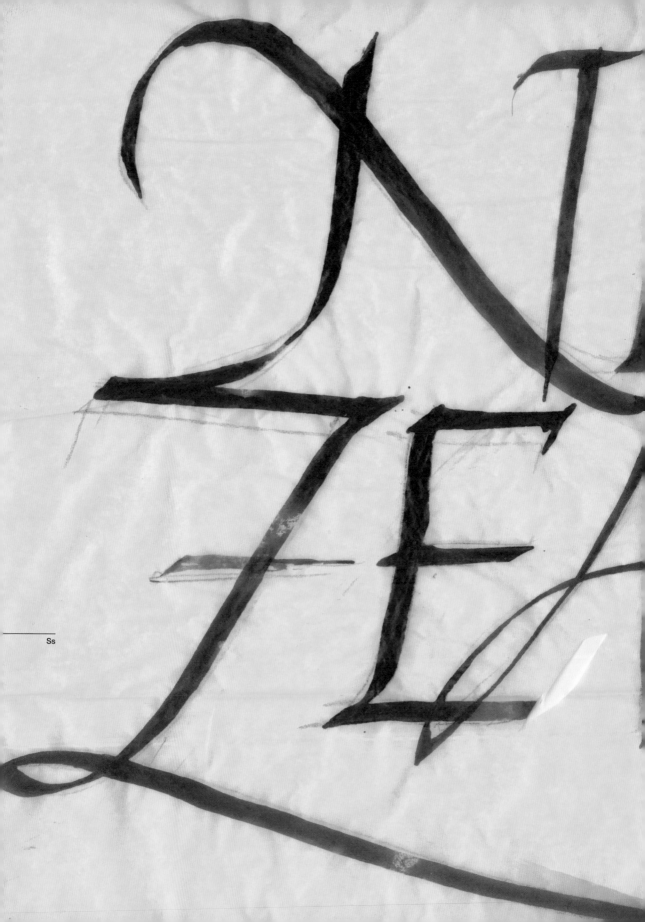

Ss

Ina Saltz

Type tattoo collector and author Ina Saltz, from New York, recalls "being fascinated by letterforms as far back as second grade. I loved making up stories about letters, each of which seemed to have a distinct personality and life. For example, the capital B was a buxom lady carrying a bag of groceries. The capital letter I was a soldier, standing at attention."

Saltz has kept sketchbooks for almost forty years: "The purpose of my sketches varies; often they are done for the sheer sensual pleasure of feeling the flow of the ink or paint from the broad edge of the pen. The deliciousness of that feeling, the doing and the watching as the magic happens, has never left me."

The pieces she loves best honor a timeworn tradition: lettering artists from all over the world send one another calligraphic keepsakes to mark the year's passing. "Perhaps what is most unique to these sketches is the use of color; I love to write with gouache, and especially on a dark ground with a light color, or gold. There is something about the quality and feeling of the paint, mixing it with an extra drop for just the right viscosity: thin enough to flow smoothly over the top of the broad-edged pen and yet produce a hairline, and thick enough to achieve the necessary opacity."

O BEAUTIFUL FOR SPA[cious]

for Amber waves of grain · for [p]

above THE fruited PLAIN!

AMERICA! AMERI[ca]

And crown thy good with BROTHERHOOD

from SEA to SHINING SEA!

O BEAUTIFUL for PILGRIM FEET

for STERN IMPASSIONED STRESS

A THOROUGHFARE of

FREEDOM BEAT across THE

AMRICA!

GOD mend THINE every FLAW thy SOUL

CONFIRM in self-control

thy LIBERTY in LAW!

O BEAUTIFUL for HEROES

PROVED IN LIBERATING STRIFE

Wo MORE than SELF their COUNTRY L[ov]

And MERCY MORE than LIFE!

AMERICA

AME[rica]

Words BY Katharine LEE BATES MELODY BY SAMUEL WARD

WITH OUR WARMEST WISHES from LISA JAMES and STEVEN

CALLIGRAPHX

BY INA SALTZ

OUS

MOUNTAIN

MAJESTIES

O! GOD SHED HIS GRACE ON THEE

DERNESS

ERICA

May GOD THY GOLD refine

TILL ALL SUCCESS BE NOBLENESS

and EVERY GAIN DIVINE

O BEAUTIFUL

for patriot DREAM that sees beyond the YEARS

Thine ALABASTER CITIES GLEAM undimmed by HUMAN TEARS

AMERICA! AMERICA!

GOD SHED HIS GRACE ON THEE

and CROWNED THY GOOD with BROTHERHOOD

from SEA to a SHINING SEA!

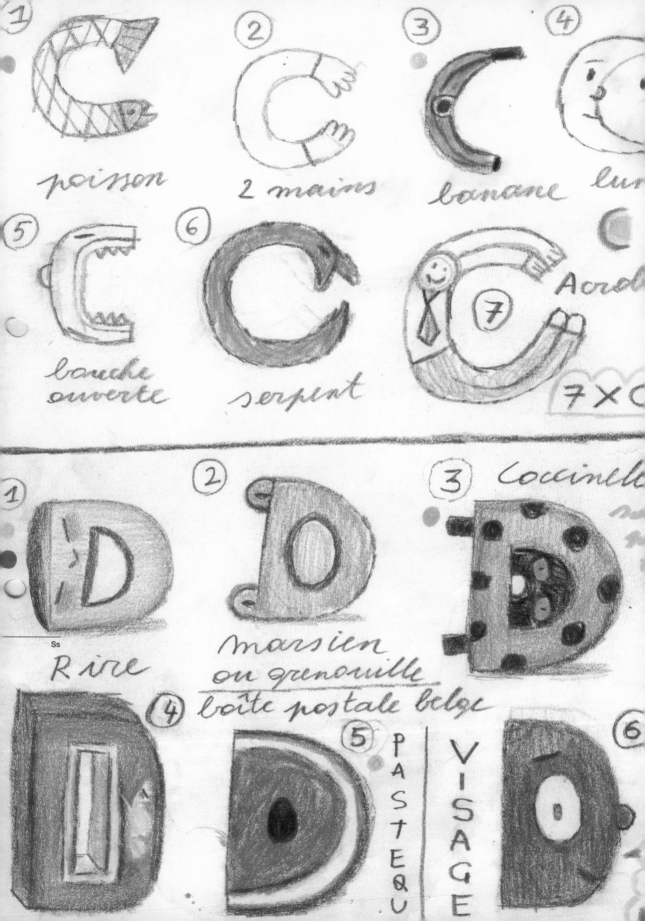

① poisson

② 2 mains

③ banane

④ lun

⑤ bouche ouverte

⑥ serpent

⑦

Acrob

7 × C

① Rire

② marsien ou grenouille

③ Coccinelle

④ boîte postale belge

⑤ PASTEQU

VISAGE

⑥

Tom Schamp

Tom Schamp is an illustrator from Brussels, Belgium, with a particular interest in hand-lettering. He has been making sketches on separate A4 sheets for twenty years. "I file them like an office clerk year after year in a binder, in chronological order," he admits with a smile. "Their only goal is to communicate with customers and my later self, so I would be able to remember what I was thinking or dreaming at a certain moment; I'm a bit of a distracted professor who forgets easily what he was planning to do in the very beginning while I'm in the process of painting." The sketches, he notes, "are in every way a prelude, but sometimes they don't have to lead to a full symphony. I usually make them without any feelings of reluctance or shame, illusions, or burdens of expectation, which I can unfortunately not always say of my finals."

The most important element is spontaneity, "which has most certainly to do with my all-time love for letters." The images shown here are from 2008 to 2009.

MAKE STUFF! ONE 9

Keith Scharwath

Los Angeles-based graphic designer, illustrator, and art director Keith Scharwath says his sketchbook "is an idea generation and storage tool. It's the first place I go when I need to create something. I also go back and mine the pages for ideas that I had earlier that might be recycled. In addition to that, I will create elements in the book which are then imported into a final piece. A lot of what I do is created right in the sketchbook." Freedom certainly reigns in his books: "I fill page after page without much consideration for composition or a narrative

of any kind, because I always compose things on the computer," he says. "I like that the random groupings of letterforms and doodles make their own secondary unintentional art piece."

From a lettering perspective, emotionally charged words and phrases, "although completely out of context here, definitely have the most impact. I wasn't thinking about it that way when I made these selections, but that seems to be what these have in common," he observes.

GASTA
AGAIN
PLAY
HAPPENING

Make
m
Something

I
om
ono
oro
orn
oro

THE
C
Born
Cry To
T Cry

THROW DOWN

the sunday KICK

REBRITH

AT THE

Soul Cleansing

Dotted Line

Helga Schmid

Helga Schmid is a Berlin-born designer and artist who says she "has planted roots in the pavement of Brooklyn, New York." Her tables, chairs, and dressers are covered with sketches.

Schmid speaks and writes with an ethereal voice: "My sketches contain what I know and perhaps what I should or want or need to remember for later. They are created without a clear goal in mind, but often lead to more. I would describe my work as very precise and clean, whereas my sketches have the freedom to be dirty, imperfect, incomplete, and ugly."

Schmid says she prefers to write in an expressive way: "I love to experiment with materials and sizes. Many of my sketches are not on paper; they can be huge and tiny. They are maybe made out of clay, written on the wall, or up in the air."

Up in the air or on the desk, with pen or feathered quill, the work here from 2010 was all related to her School of Visual Arts MFA Design thesis project. No drawings at all; just cursive script of writing she adores.

m says,
d still.
s paint-
you a
face!"

This day
marks some
kind of
new
beginning

a b c d e f g
h i j k l m n
o p r s t u v
w x y z &

A B C D E F G
H I J K L M N
O P Q R S T U
V W X Y Z

Revolution Tullahoma
Sammy Gulley and Friends
Rock and Roll Forever
Boston Nashville Express
Moore County Mavericks
Infatuated Isfahan Xray

Carlos Segura

Chicago-based Carlos Segura, founder of the T26 type foundry, came to the United States from Cuba at the age of nine. He worked for numerous high-profile advertising agencies, including BBDO, Marsteller, Foote Cone & Belding, Young & Rubicam, Ketchum, and DDB Needham, before founding Segura Inc. in 1991. This family of custom fonts for the Jack Daniel's whiskey label was created by Segura along with Rod Cavazos (see page 60).

For the project, the three prominent lettering styles from the famous Black Label (c.1904) were developed into complete fonts. The main lettering is Jasper font (opposite, top), based on the familiar Jack Daniel's logo lettering. The real visual centerpiece, though, is the refined yet approachable Lynchburg Script, based on the Tennessee lettering in the label (above and opposite, bottom). Rounding out the set is the solid, industrious typeface named for Lem Motlow, the nephew of Jack Daniel who managed and later inherited the Distillery.

Leanne Shapton

From New York, Leanne Shapton, art director, illustrator, author and publisher, creates faux and real book covers using hand-lettering and patterns as her primary conceit. As the co-founder, with photographer Jason Fulford, of J&L Books, an internationally distributed not-for-profit imprint, she specializes in art and photography titles. In 2006 she published a book in pictures, *Was She Pretty?*, and in 2009 *Important Artifacts and Personal Property from the Collection of Lenore Doolan and Harold Morris, Including*

Books, Street Fashion and Jewelry, a satiric auction catalog that tells the story of a nasty relationship break-up.

Shapton's work is quite loose, so her sketches "resemble my finished work very closely." But "most of them are cut off mid-word," she notes. "I like language to be a peripheral yet strong presence in images. I make sketchbooks in certain places I travel to, and I will paint the place and date on the cover of the sketchbook. I'll also do that by month. I suppose the larger themes are always time or place."

Ss

LONDON /LUCCA JULY 2009

MUS- TIQ- UE

JANUARY 2010

#66
B
width: 4:

Paul Shaw

Paul Shaw is a calligrapher, typographer, and noted type scholar in New York. His notebooks "are full of sketches of letters by other people rather than sketches of original letters or doodles," he confides. "They contain drawings of letters I have found in books, libraries, museums, cemeteries, etc. Many are calligraphic but others are from letters that have been drawn or carved. The purpose of the sketchbooks has been as both an *aide-mémoire* and as a resource."

"I often recorded letters that showed ingenious or unusual solutions to problems such as imaginative ligatures or swashes," Shaw adds. "When I began designing typefaces in the 1990s these sketchbooks became the basis for both Kolo and the Florentine Set. The process I went through in designing Kolo and Donatello (the main font in the Florentine Set) was to copy out all of my relevant sketches, choose examples of letters that I liked best from each group, redraw them to a common height and weight, invent missing letters (as well as figures and punctuation) and then hand the alphabet to my partner Garrett Boge for digitizing."

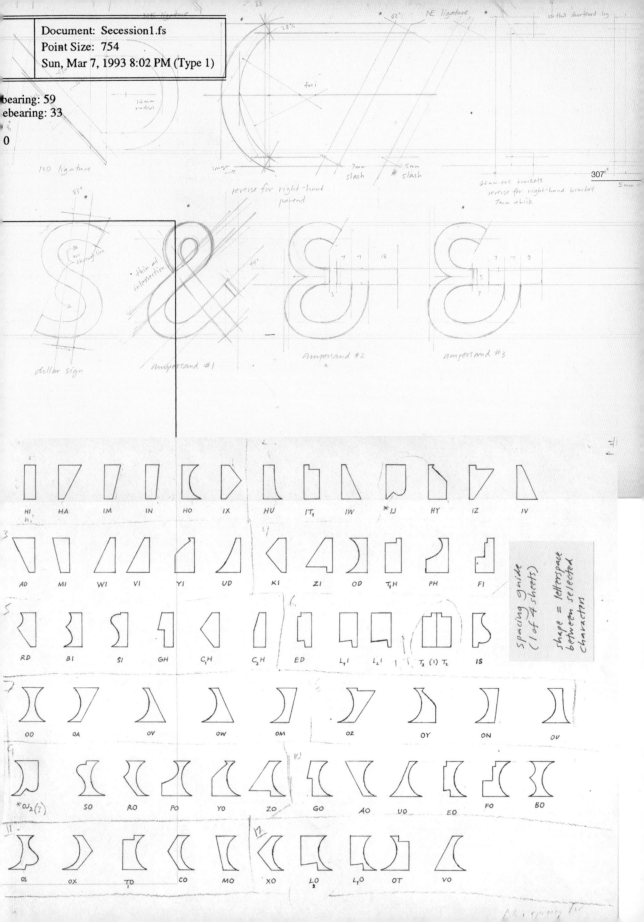

Document: Secession1.fs
Point Size: 754
Sun, Mar 7, 1993 8:02 PM (Type 1)

bearing: 59
ebearing: 33

0

A A A A A B B

← drop one of
these for
narrow
A

flare insides of legs; flatten 'feet'   crotch may
be necessary

more optical adjustment?   see page 1
Paul Sanding 'drooping'   add narrow D and bottom heavy D

C C C C C D D E

replace
with
fig. 7 C ?   more stem
weight

smoother

very slight flare?

more optical adjustment   see pg. 4 (drooping)   more stem weight
longer   3. Wider
on this   1, add narrower   2. wider on this

G G G G H H H I

see Ⓐ

more stem
weight   more stem weight
for all H's

5/22/93

add the extra
flare   flare
weight on the outside   add with...revision
# of this N   heavier stem   *

N N M N E G O   *
see
pg 2

w/
added weight flare   flare on outside   flare on outside   deleted bar on jaw;
heavier stem   more weight on
interior of sides?

match "O"counter
also see Q   (Q dropped)   adding 4 to R

P P Q Q Q R R R

shorter

steeper   flare   ?   slight
curvature
here

stress on interior sides   stress on interior sides;
tail moved up & to right   longer
for
QU   flare   more weight to stems of all R's & flattened feet on

wider   also smaller   flatten   flare   narrower

S T T S U U U

flatter
cut-off   ?   heavier
stem

smooth
curves

add weight
to stems of T's

add one of new W's see page 2 (W)   * check symmetry

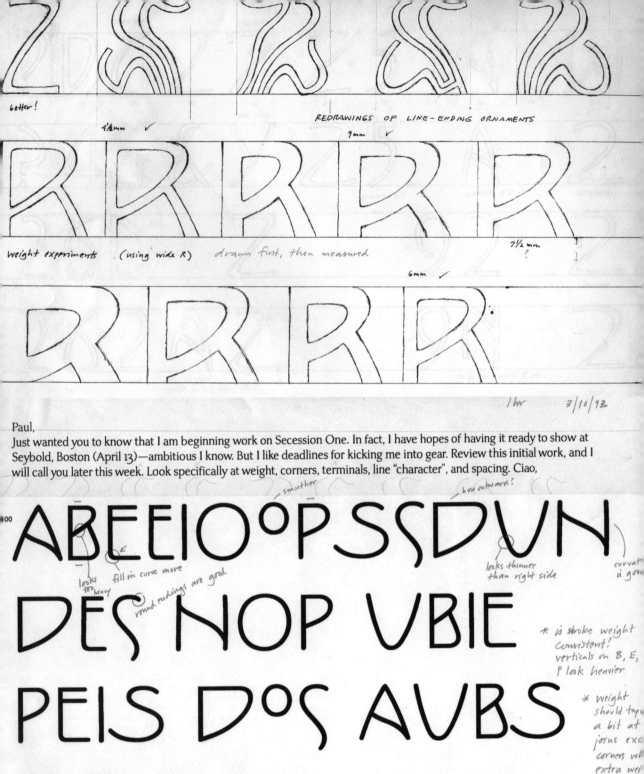

better!

REDRAWINGS OF LINE-ENDING ORNAMENTS

4½mm ✓   9mm ✓

weight experiments   (using wide R)   drawn first, then measured   7½mm ?

6mm ✓

1 hr   3/10/93

Paul,
Just wanted you to know that I am beginning work on Secession One. In fact, I have hopes of having it ready to show at Seybold, Boston (April 13)—ambitious I know. But I like deadlines for kicking me into gear. Review this initial work, and I will call you later this week. Look specifically at weight, corners, terminals, line "character", and spacing. Ciao,

smoother

bow outward?

ABEEIOºPSSDUN

looks too heavy   fill in curve more   round endings are good   looks thinner than right side   curvature is good

DEŞ NOP VBIE

* is stroke weight consistent? verticals on B, E, P look heavier

PEIS DºŞ AVBS

* weight should taper a bit at joins except corners where extra weight needed for "swing"

100/50 ABEEIOºPSSDUN DEŞ NOP VBIE PEIS DºŞ AVBS

30/30 ABEEIOºPSSDUN DEŞ NOP VBIE PEIS DºŞ AVBS

← taper

7 March 1993

"swing"

16
heavier

A B C D

H I J K L

P Q R R

W X Y

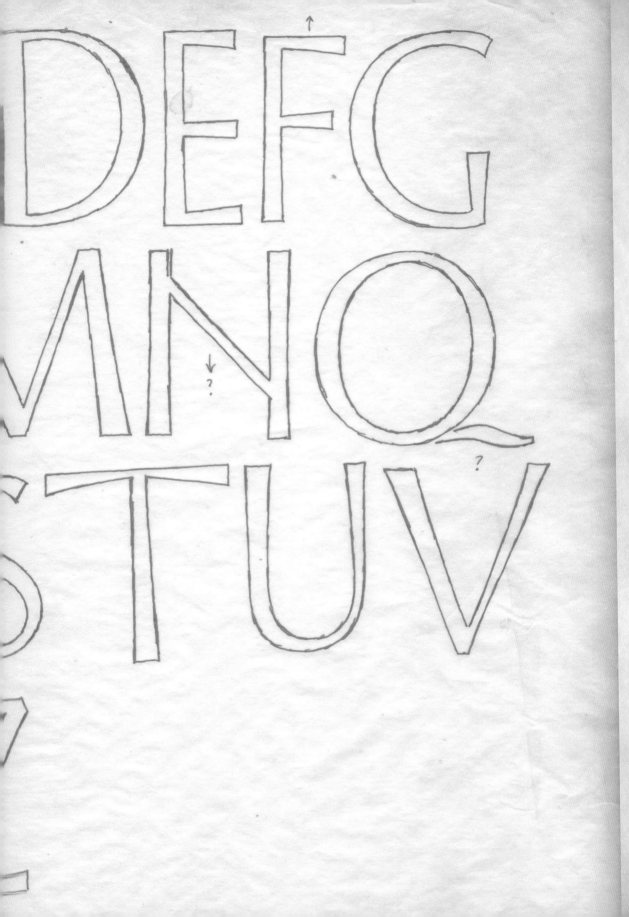

Andy Smith

London-based designer and hand-letterer Andy Smith says, "When I first went to college in London I used to try and draw everything I could, including signs, bits of conversations heard, everything. A lot of these images used to find their way into finished pieces, or give me ideas for books/stories. As my work started to take me in a different direction, away from drawing from life, they became a little more like notebooks, so I'd just write things down or maybe doodle an idea but not draw it as such. Now they are somewhere in between these two things."

The sketches can be for a final piece, or musings without an end purpose. "Some of the things I note down I know will never lead to anything but might spark another thought some day." When asked if he has any thematic strains in his books, Smith emphatically notes, "Not really. I am interested in creating work that is very immediate, clear, and that shouts a bit, and that is reflected in the phrases I am drawn to. I like the headlines, not the body copy!"

Erik Spiekermann

Berlin-based Erik Spiekermann is an information architect, type designer, and author. He was founder in 1979 of MetaDesign and designed the faces FF Meta, FF Meta Serif, ITC Officina, FF Govan, FF Info, FF Unit, LoType and Berliner Grotesk, and many corporate typefaces. In 1988 he started FontShop, which produces and distributes electronic fonts. Among his honors, he was made an Honorary Royal Designer for Industry by the RSA in the UK in 2007 and Ambassador for the European Year of Creativity and Innovation by the European Union for 2009.

He has been keeping notebooks for about fifteen years. They are mainly for storing ideas and concepts (more writing than drawing), but also for first sketches for typefaces, or alternatives for letters already existing as print-outs from digital files. "It is easier to prove a point by drawing over a print than changing a file," he says.

His sketchbooks are quick and dirty: "No finish, no data, no grid." What's more, he notes, "I am always surprised how rough they are, but also how ideas are still captured and how designers communicate with each other using even the simplest sketches."

Included here are FF Meta (above and overleaf, right), DB Type for Deutsche Bahn (opposite, top, and overleaf, left), and a design for the Museum Folkwang in Essen (right).

eFolkwang

eFolkwang

kg

gerechte

Kontrast
nach links

Alternativen

ang
rs anaa

Außenkontur
wie Meta
Book

MetaSerif
02/02

Serifen im Winkel?
kräftig, fast Slab
(Candida etc)

Plantin?

22
+ 1,5
27,5

Hed

gerade

5
10 11

gerade?

DB Serif
15·07·09

flachen

schmaler

steiler nach unten

Beule weg!

1. Version
15·1·85

etwas runder

← runder

flacher

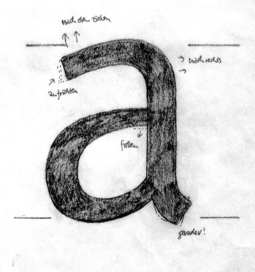

nach oben ziehen

nach rechts

aufrichten

füllen

gerader!

1. Version – 15. Januar '85

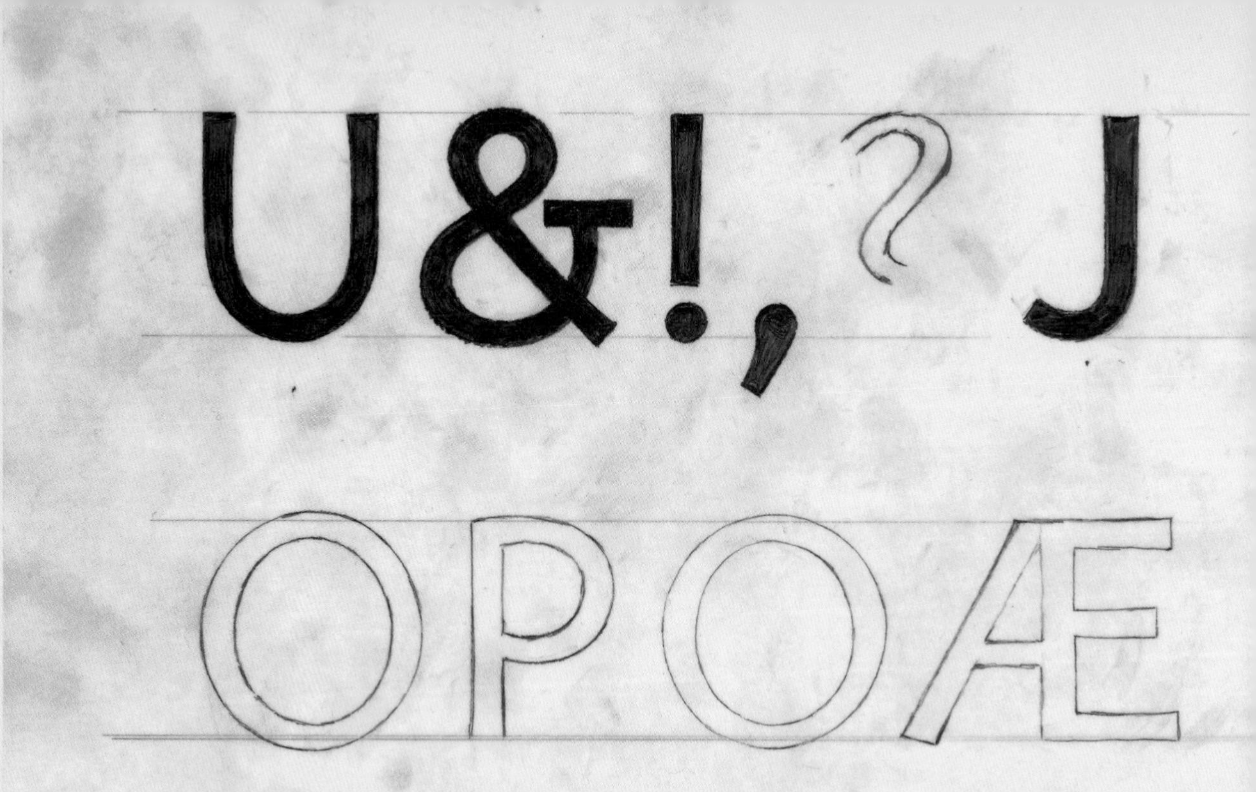

U & ᴛ ! , ‽ J

OPOÆ

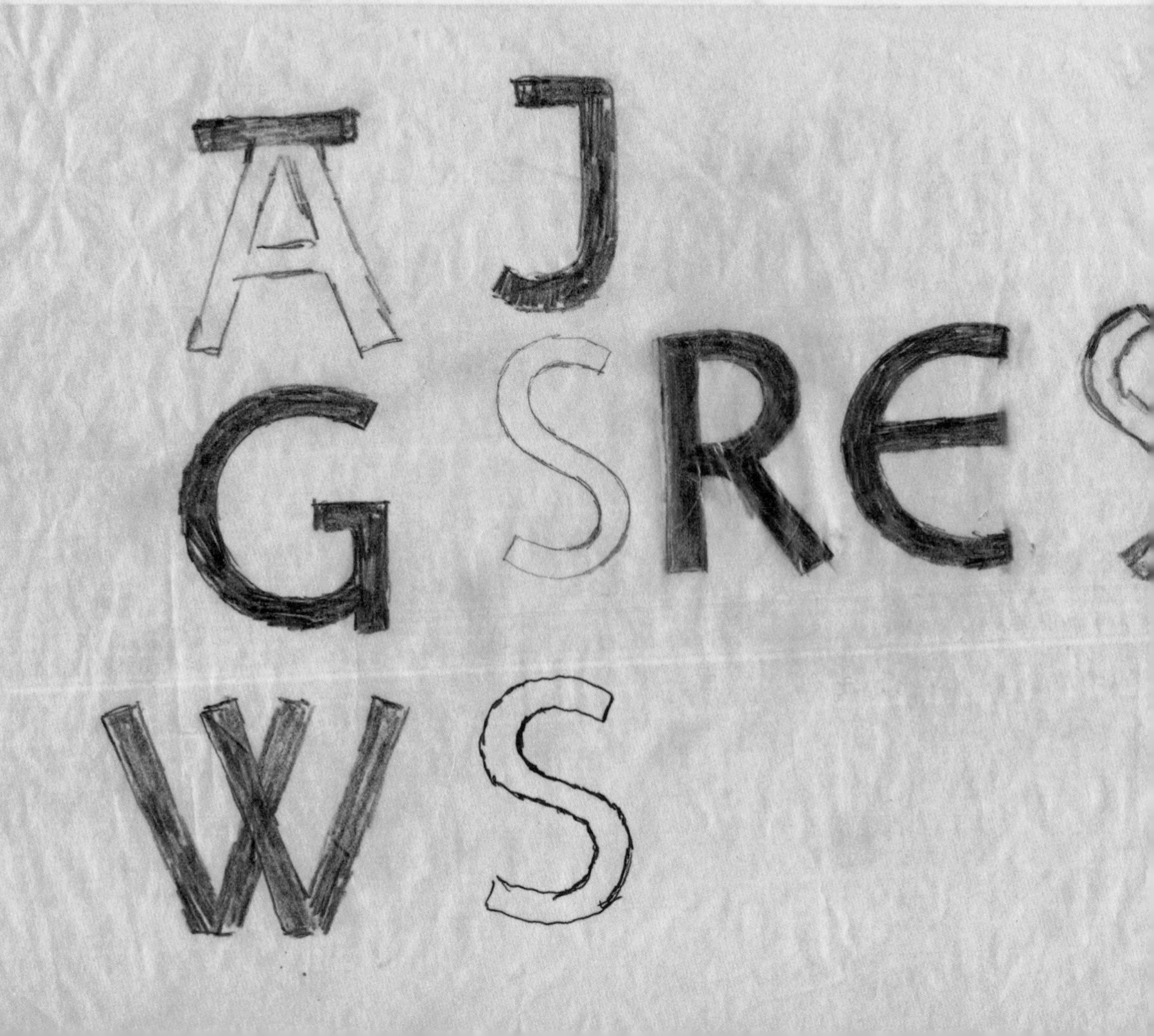

A J
G S R E S
W S

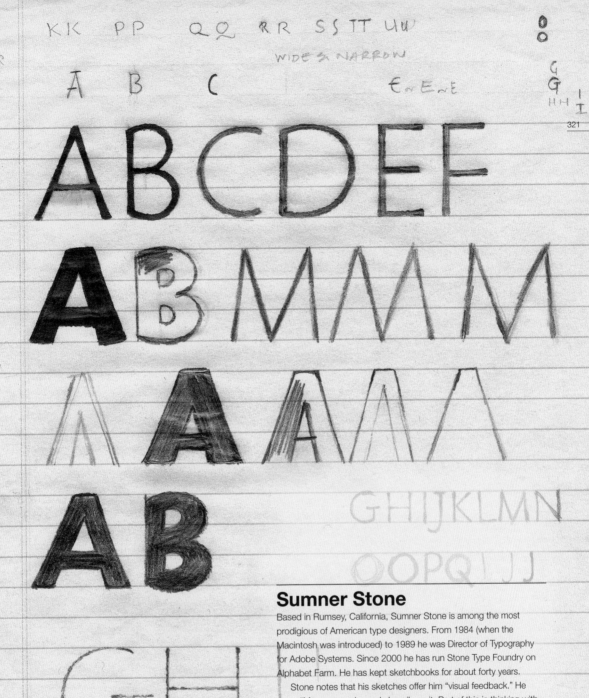

Sumner Stone

Based in Rumsey, California, Sumner Stone is among the most prodigious of American type designers. From 1984 (when the Macintosh was introduced) to 1989 he was Director of Typography for Adobe Systems. Since 2000 he has run Stone Type Foundry on Alphabet Farm. He has kept sketchbooks for about forty years.

Stone notes that his sketches offer him "visual feedback." He says, "My process depends heavily on it. Part of this is thinking with the pen or pencil. Sometimes the hand seems to know things that are not conscious, and the act of drawing allows these to emerge. Also, the activity of making the sketches creates an environment that seems to promote creative thinking."

His sketches go through various stages. "These sketches for Basalt/Magma/Munc were done at the beginning of projects that went on for several years, and the ideas for the type designs were in a formative stage. Many more drawings were made along with much more thinking and planning before the organization and structure of these related typeface families was worked out."

STENCIL

Patrick Thomas

Patrick Thomas makes politically themed illustrations and posters
at his Studio LaVista in Barcelona, Spain. He started keeping
sketchbooks during his first year at Central Saint Martins College of
Art & Design in London in the 1980s. The early books were large-
format discarded ledgers that he found in a skip (aka trash can) in the
street one day. Since that time he has always had a book on the go.

"I have a memory like a sieve," he says. "The sketches are my
visual diary, they feed my work. If I'm feeling uninspired, a quick
thumb through a sketchbook will usually help kick-start an idea.
When I'm sketching I'm not thinking about a final piece. Sometimes
it is nice to scribble without feeling obliged to make a point."

Typographically, Thomas includes "lots of handwriting and
drawing. Also I enjoy rendering letterforms, which rarely manifest
themselves in my finished work." Sketches appeal to him for their
spontaneity. "As they are for my own reference, I'm not concerned
about polishing. These images are taken from a collection of travel
sketchbooks, and when I'm on the move I find the lack of studio
equipment very liberating," he explains.

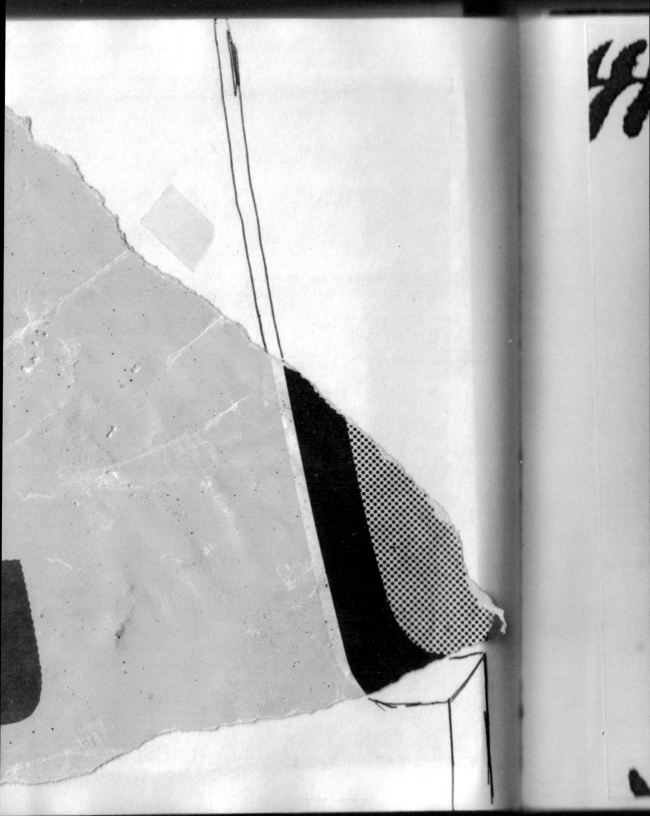

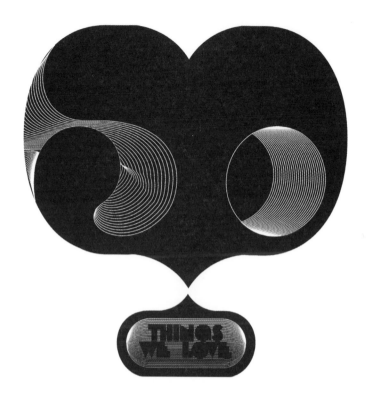

Alex Trochut

Barcelona-based illustrator and typographer
Alex Trochut says he "takes the modern
notion of minimalism and flips it on its side."
Perhaps he throws it on its back, too.
His illuminated lettering underscores the
alternative theory that "more is more" and
then more again. His work is self-described
as "rich with elegant, brilliantly detailed
executions that simultaneously convey
indulgence and careful, restrained control."
That control is not an illusion.

Trochut's eccentric sketches, which
he retains for almost every job he does
for a lengthy list of clients from Absolut to
Zune, prove the essence of his intense but
nonetheless curiously restrained exactitude.
And such amazing craft is required to make
these come alive.

Included here are the cover for *Disappear
Here* magazine (the "50 Things We Love"
issue), black-and-white type illustration of
the letter S, which had to represent the
Street Skateboarding (S-Kate) brand by
using urban elements, and a 2009 front
and back cover design in collaboration
with Non-Format for *Varoom* magazine.

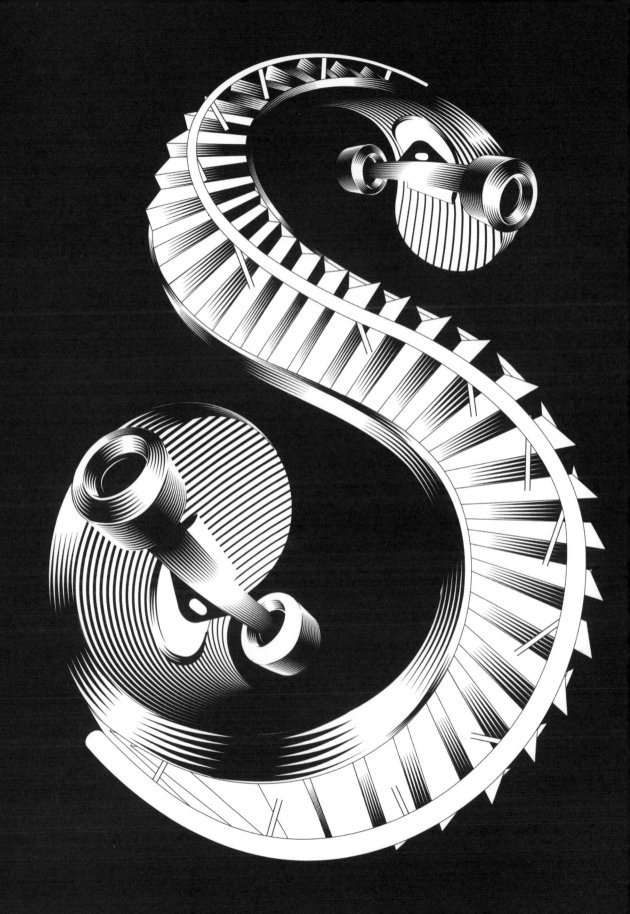

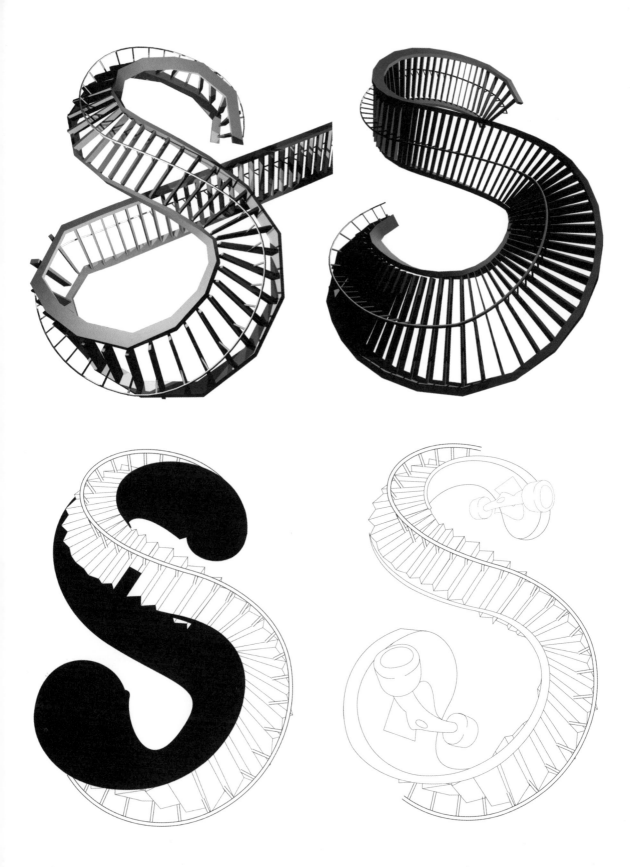

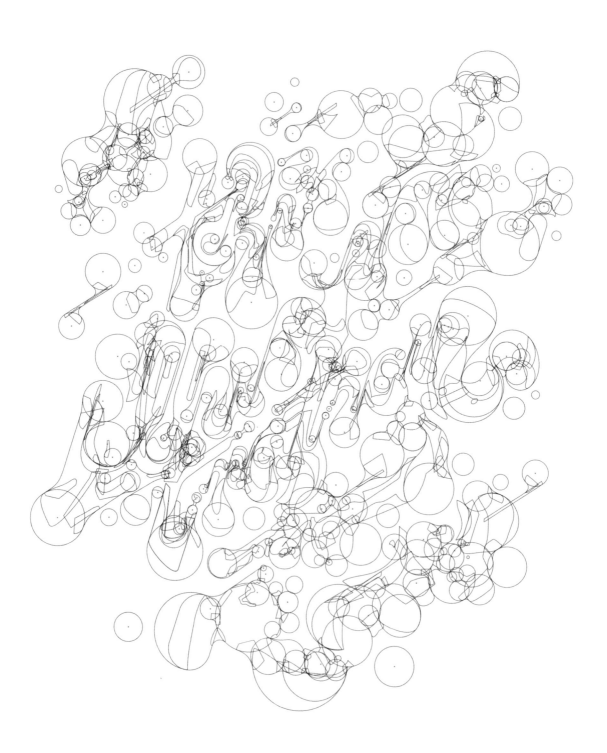

Rick Valicenti

Rick Valicenti formed Thirst in Chicago in 1989. Known for his early adoption of technology, his approach to digital tools has been to accentuate the play principle. In 2005 his work "Intelligent Design," a commentary on the "religion of commerce," employed programming tools to convert the Book of Genesis to binary code, and then replace the 0s and 1s with an image of either Coke or Pepsi. He has since used this program to collect and place large numbers of images in other projects, and continues to scour the universe for technologies he can bend to the designer's hand.

His sketchbook practice has been in force just over thirty years. "My sketches are usually very fast records of those pesky fleeting moments," he says; "the stuff that is never accessible or within reach the morning after." He adds that "mostly my recent books are filled with the stuff of life and observation rather than thumbnails for professional commission. They represent the lack of precision and exist on pages where there are no unlimited undos or 0.25-point incremental composition shifts. And they seem to be the aesthetic of my subconscious."

He insists that for the most part "my sketchbooks are a handy version of flypaper ... usually they collect the things seen and overheard."

LA MAGIA TRAGICA MAS EXTRAERDINARIA

Vv

Laura Varsky

Laura Varsky, an illustrator and graphic designer from Buenos Aires, Argentina, made her first leap into the design world through her involvement with the local independent rock scene before specializing in book and CD design. Following ten years teaching typography at the University of Buenos Aires School of Design, she now lectures throughout Latin America and Spain. Sketching is important to her: "I make my sketches before I make a specific illustration. I need to do it," she asserts. "It's the only way that the images of my mind can

become alive: line by line." Varsky also insists the sketches are not just for pleasure. "I can't draw without an end purpose. You can see how my hand is searching for something. I love to see that. I don't know if I can say there is an 'unusual' quality to the sketches, but there is something that you can't see in a final work: the wrong lines almost deleted, but visible there, on paper."

What she likes most about her sketches, the ones here from 2005, is making letters, flowers, "and plenty of whimsicality."

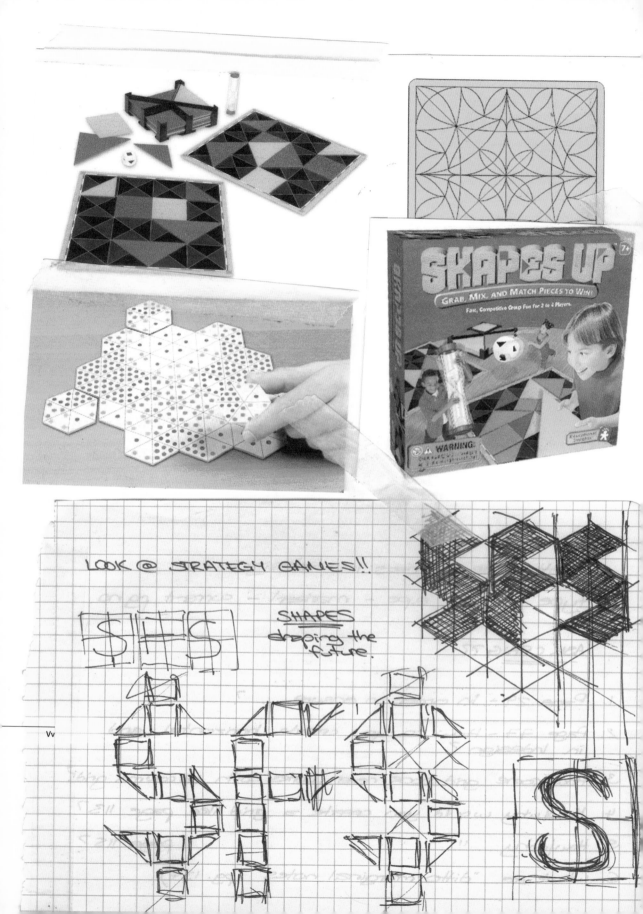

LOOK @ STRATEGY GAMES!!

SHAPES
shaping the future.

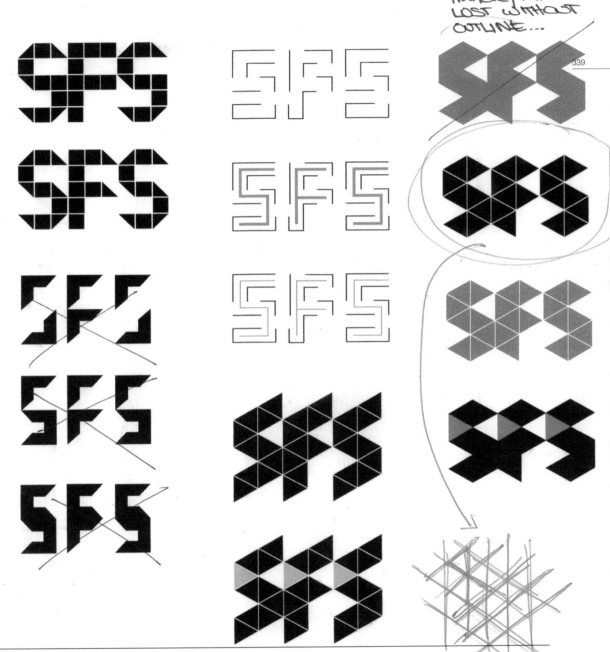

Tiana Vasiljev

Born in Subotica, Serbia, and currently based in London, the peripatetic Vasiljev graduated from the Enmore Design Centre, Sydney, Australia. She began her design career in 2007 but began keeping a sketchbook when she was twelve. "I have kept every sketchbook I have ever owned. I am constantly surprised at what you can find by simply flipping through an old sketchbook. There is nothing as comforting as turning a page and having a blank sheet to fill; a fresh new page to stick things onto. I could never begin my projects by heading straight to the computer."

Vasiljev collects posters, drawings, prints, letters, photographs, and signs. She is fascinated by typography, letters, words, and patterns, and her sketchbooks are primarily filled with typographic experiments, whether it be for a branding project or a new typeface. "My sketchbooks are also filled with collected images of typefaces, inspirational quotes, and lists of recommended design books, magazines, websites, or documentaries. They help me to stimulate new ideas."

She adds, "You need to have a different perspective for every client, and I find the best way to do this is to create word lists, mind maps, mood boards, to scribble and collect images somehow related to that particular project. As a result, the majority of my pages are progressive sketches that lead to my final concept or design."

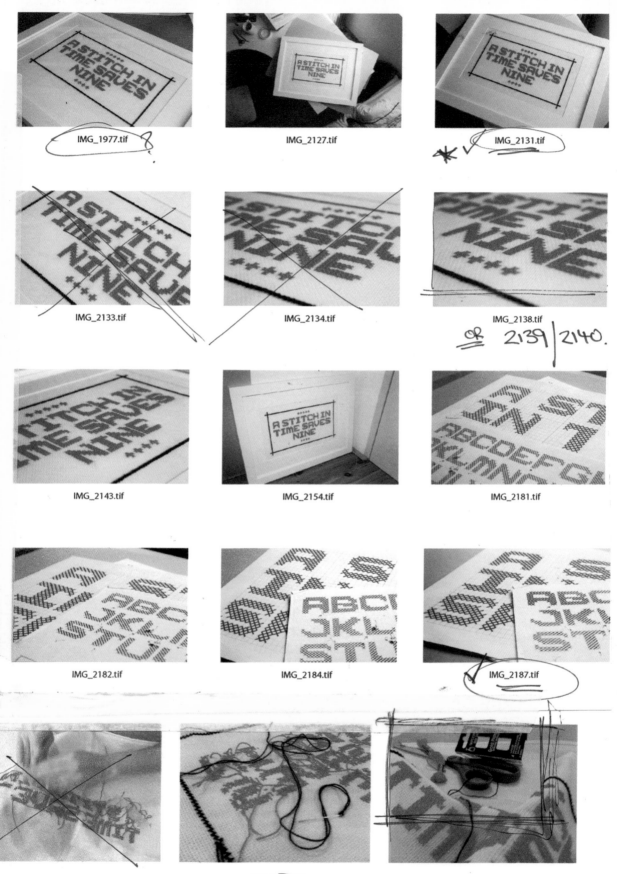

IMG_1977.tif

IMG_2127.tif

IMG_2131.tif

IMG_2133.tif

IMG_2134.tif

IMG_2138.tif

OR 2139/2140.

IMG_2143.tif

IMG_2154.tif

IMG_2181.tif

IMG_2182.tif

IMG_2184.tif

IMG_2187.tif

IMG_0075.tif

IMG_0126.tif

IMG_0140.tif

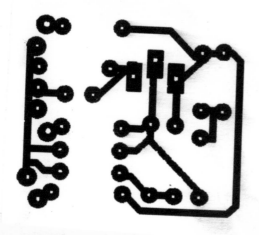

TOO-SIMPLE
NOW ??

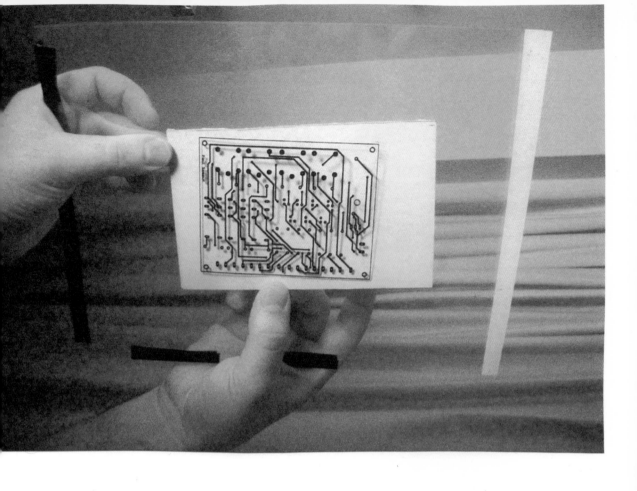

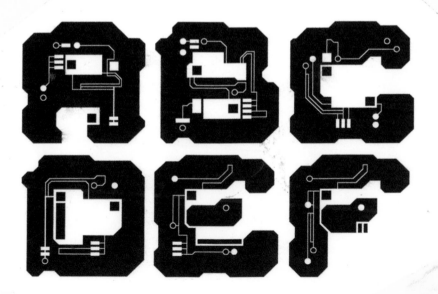

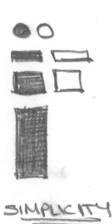

SIMPLICITY

Leigh Wells

Leigh Wells is an illustrator and letterer now based in San Francisco, who has avidly kept sketchbooks "for as long as I can remember, but probably began engaging more seriously in them during college. When I look back, I see the best work is drawings of the insides of airports and airplanes. Being trapped seems to help."

Wells keeps project-based sketchbooks for her illustration work, but her personal sketchbooks are purely for entertainment. "This one was to collect bits of typography I wanted to remember from trips to San Francisco, signs near my studio in New York, and a few bits from Portland, Oregon," she says. "These sketches really focus on the forms and color and the pleasure of seeing/finding. Unlike my illustration work, they don't have to communicate anything or have a purpose other than to please me. All of it is based in what I encounter, ready-made in front of me, the only interpretation being my hand and an editing of what to depict." These images are probably from 2001 to 2002, Wells's last two years in New York.

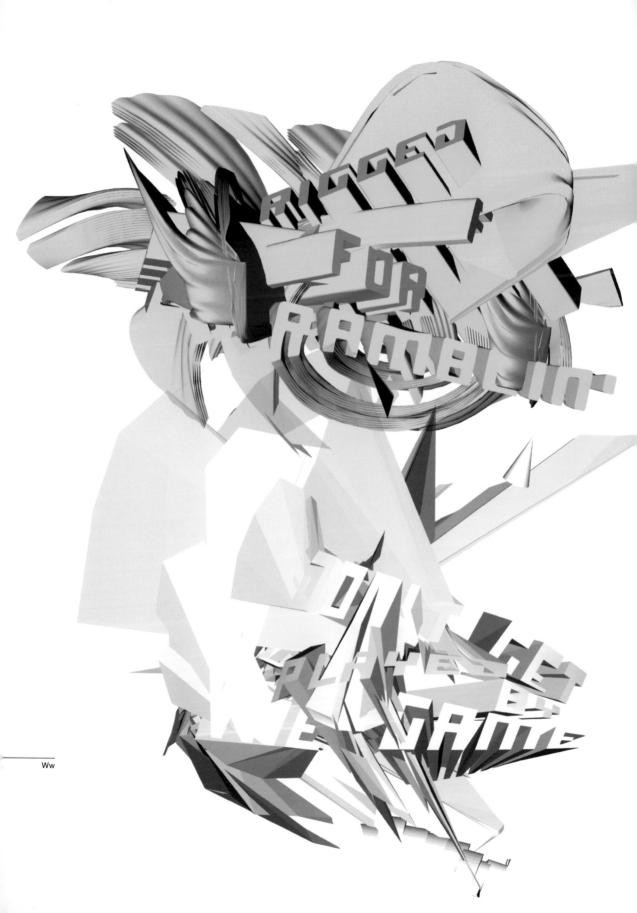

RIGGED FOR RAMBLIN'

DON'T THER PUBLISHED BY ENDGAME

Ww

MUSEUM
UND
OFFEN

IJKL
MNOPQ
THE RSTU
MUSEUM OF
MOVING
ADMISSION
GALLERY

Jan Wilker

Jan Wilker grew up in Ulm, Germany, and graduated from the State Academy of Art and Design in Stuttgart. Today his New York studio with Hjalti Karlsson, karlssonwilker inc., creates unconventional approaches to conventional assignments. His drawing pen and pencil are covered in mothballs and his sketchbook is the computer: "So long as I have had a computer (which is always), I have had a sketchbook. I save the sketches, but I don't use that feature to go back and revisit old sketches," he says.

The purpose of sketching – on the computer – is to "guide me to an end of the process. Sometimes they will survive until the end, sometimes not. What is unique to these sketches is the amount of hours put into details – sometimes not visible to anyone but me."

When asked what is the single most unusual aspect of these images, Wilker boastfully replied: "Nothing unusual."

ABCDEFGHIJK
LMNOPQRS
TUVWXYZ
abcdefghijkl
mnopqrstuv
wxyz
1234567890

Charles Wilkin

Charles Wilkin, proprietor of the Brooklyn-based Automatic Art and Design, doesn't keep a traditional sketchbook. Instead he prefers to make piles and to fill files full of thoughts and works in progress scattered around his studio. "I like to live with my work in plain view; it really helps me motivate," he says.

Wilkin uses his sketches either to document a spontaneous idea or as an experimental outlet. "Sometimes if I have a creative urge at, like, 2 a.m., I will do sketches to just get that energy out of my system," he reveals. "However, sometimes they do end up being finished into a final piece or project, but that is not the norm for me. I think too much expectation in the beginning can really kill your inspiration."

Of course, sketches are just quick thoughts, not polished, final work. "Sketches are where my ideas are more free-form and could easily be titled 'a work in progress.' Each sketch is a moment in time, a place or a feeling. Perhaps if you look at my sketches over time you could see a more distinct theme or pattern, but that would really be completely unintentional."

Ww

dfahygubluj

vxkkıiczr

AA Waid

NNLG

XTHOY

ABCDEFGHI

AMSTERDAM 2008

AMSTERDAM HEEMSTEDE

THE NETHERLANDS THE WORLD

STOP DE MEER KOEM IN DE WOMBAT

ROSENTHEATHER + K. EDIRIES MAN
02 207. EI

IKSTER ZIERIKZEE DOPESTYLERS

EXODUS ALUMINIUM AHARON

GENSUS OPUS SCHOOL'S OUT SER

GROTESKISKI DUITSER RUSLAND

DIEDERIK ZELDA A.M.S.DK

Ww

CREATIVE

1. HORSE PERMANENT MARKER – ASTM D4236

REVIEW

2. DA VINCI BRUSH №16 – SERIE 18 / TALENS INDIAN INK

CREATIVE

3. EDDING 550 PERMANENT MARKER

REVIEW

4. UNI POSCA BRUSH MARKER 3-24

CREATIVE

5. HEMA (KIDS) MARKER

REVIEW

6. PENTEL COLOR BRUSH FR-X101

LETMAN·09

Job Wouters

Job Wouters (aka Letman) is a designer, illustrator, typographer, and massive doodler from Amsterdam. His hand-lettered graphics are eccentric, eclectic, and passionately excessive.

Wouters started drawing on an almost daily basis when he was fifteen. "I have a huge archive of drawings from that period," he proudly expounds. "Both sketchbooks and loose papers, mostly graffiti drawings." He asserts that drawing is a means of relaxation, "and while I'm having a good time I'm also training my hand and doing research on new materials, letterforms, or scripts." He adds, "I used to feel bad about those piles of doodles in my house and at my studio. I found it a waste of time. But lately I see that it is in fact an important part of my professional practice. I would say most of it is research and development."

Repetition in his books is something he enjoys. "My attempt to master some script, for example, takes pages and pages. I think this is my way. The progress goes slow but steady."

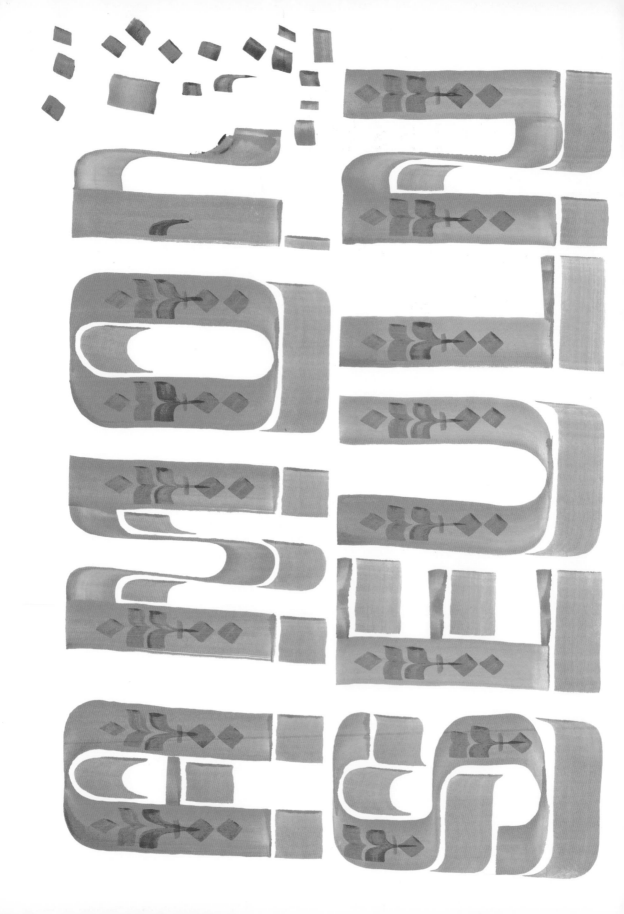

LIFE'S TOO SHORT FOR REGRETS

- WHY IS THERE ALWAYS AN ASSHOLE IN CHARGE?
- DO CHOPSTICKS WORK IN MEXICO?
- DOES BIGFOOT LOVE
- DO HAIR PLUGS MAKE YOU SEXY?

THE POTATOE IS ██ A REPUBLICAN DELICACY. BLTS. ARE WEAPONS OF ██ASS REDUCTIONS. OPRAH WINFREY ██ CONTROLS ██ JERRY SPRINGER ██ WITH OXYCONTON. RUSH LIMBOUGH IS HIS OWN WORST ENEMA. THOMAS KINCALD ██ IS THE DONALD RUMSFELD OF CARSLCURO. ██ ██ BLISTERS ARE FUH OF MAGIC JUICE. EVEN TERRORISTS LIKE ICE-CREAM. HUMMERS ██ RUN ON HAIR PLUGS AND VIAGRA.

IS SPACE MOUNTAIN HOME TO? BIGFOOT
DOES RALPH NADER
DO HAIR PLUGS
ARE

Q's IS JANET JACKSONS TITTY AL QVEDA?
~~ARE TOLE HAVES THE~~
ARE DOCKERS COCK-BLOCKERS?
~~WHY DO DOES~~ 'S BIGFOOT REALLY A VEGETERIAN?
~~DO LAWYERS~~

RALPH TURD PARTY

- THEY HAVE KILLED HIM 7 TIMES, BUT HE IS BIONIC. HE RUNS ON PRUNE JUICE AND GOOGLE.

  RALPH ONCE MUD-WRESTLED TED KENNEDY FOR A USED-CAR.

  ~~RE~~ HE COULD TAKE A JOKE. BUT HE COULDN'T TAKE A BRIBE.

  HE INVENTED THE HUMAN AIR-BAG, BUT IT WAS RE-CALLED.

NADER Turd Party

- NOT EVERBODY KNOWS THAT RALPH IS ~~BIONIC~~. HE CAN RUN A CAMPAIGN ON 60.⁴
  ~~HE WAS ARRESTED FOR~~
- IF HE DROVE A PINTO TODA HE WOULD BE ARRESTED FOR TERRORISM.
- ~~HE IS THE SWAMI OF RECYCLING CULT.~~ THEY'RE CALLED
- HE HAS HIS OWN ARMY OF

THEY ③   BOTOX & ZOMBYS

MAD COW IS A VEGAN'S WEST NILE. DONALD TRUMP INVENTED THE YARD SALE. CROP CIRCLES ARE MADE BY JOHN DEERE. HAIR PLUGS MAKE YOU LOOK MORE NATURAL. THE LOVE HANDLE IS A TOOL OF THE MAN. THE BOTOX COMPANY IS CREATING A RACE OF STYLISH ZOMBIES, THAT SMILE. SATELLITES KNOW HOW MUCH MONEY YOU HAVE. COLIN POWELL IS THE HO MAN. CABS BUILT A

Yee-Haw Industries

Julie Belcher and Kevin Bradley, owners of the Knoxville, Tennessee-based Yee Haw design and print shop, create woodtype posters in the tradition of old carnival and show posters. Their sketches comprise a loose collection of paper that is stored all over the place in flat files, in piles lying about the studio – what the Yee Haw principals call a "space-age sketchbook of a working letterpress studio," but this creates "storage problems."

The purpose for these sketches varies: "Sometimes they are traditional thumbnails/roughs to flesh out ideas, or sometimes we just create the forms straight out of our typography collection," says Belcher. "Sometimes we spend a lot of time at the drafting table drawing typography, layers, shadows, color separations in a variety of methods: ink, scratchboard, woodcut, even a Mac – God help me, I said that."

The common thread in the sketch work shown here, created between 2000 and the present, is "real letterpress type from the 1700s and 1800s combined with our own drawn fonts, headlines, copy, and illustration carved into blocks," she says.

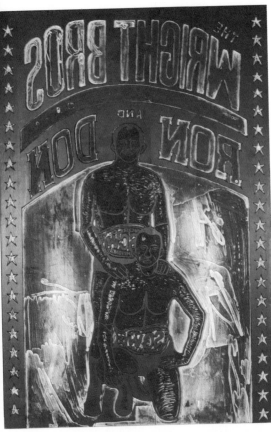

Doyald Young

Los Angeles-based typeface and logo designer Doyald Young, author of *Logo Type & Letterforms: Handlettered Logotypes and Typographic Considerations* (1993) and *Dangerous Curves: Mastering Logotype Design* (2008) is a true master of type design art and craft. He specializes in logos, corporate alphabets, and complete custom fonts for popular consumption. His typefaces include Home Run Script, Home Run Sanscript, Young Finesse, Young Baroque and Young Gallant. Having the name "Young" certainly provides his types with a fresh brand. He gives the phrase "to be young again" new resonance.

His sketches are decidedly fresh, too. "They are explorations to decide which is the best direction," he notes. Yet when asked whether he relies on accidents in making fresh Young faces, he responds, "Forethought only. I think accidents occur in handwritten forms. While hurriedly written scripts are dependent on a plan, the pen or brush may react in unanticipated ways, the ink or gouache may produce different results depending on its viscosity, and even the paper can influence the outcome depending on its texture. The speed and angle of the brush or pen may also offer surprises. And never forget that our moods are variable and may influence the results."

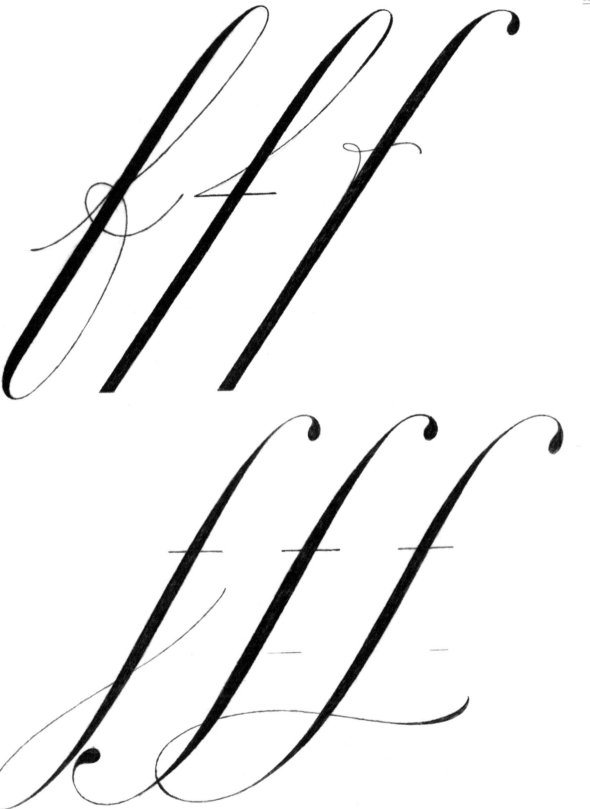

K L M N O P

Q R S T U V

W X Y Z C A

O Q G W Z I

S S L U P S

S W A M

A B C D E

F G H I I K

L M N O P

Q R S T U

V W X Y W

Z Z Z G A M

deep tight

deep tight

deep tight

deep tight

روح الشرق

روح الشرق

روح الشرق

الهاه الهاه

Zz

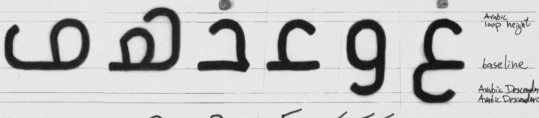

Pascal Zoghbi

Pascal Zoghbi is the founder of 29letters, an Arabic type design and typography firm in Beirut, Lebanon. His practice is based on making new Arabic fonts, corporate identities, and print publications.

"I keep all my sketchbooks in my library," he says. "I never throw them away. I change a sketchbook around every six months or so. It is a means of communication between my head, hands and eyes," he adds. "Drawing and visualizing thoughts makes them realistic and they trigger other ideas and concepts until the final stage is achieved. I always start a project by sketching and experimenting with different design alternatives until I am satisfied with a strong idea. Then I move to the computer and develop the final design. If I am doing sketches for a job, they end in a final, but sometimes I just sketch personal stuff for my own satisfaction."

Zoghbi concludes, "Sketching has the humanistic, hand-drawn spirit that can be lost when the final is digitized. Personally, I value the sketches more than the final outcome."

WEBSITES

Steven Heller is co-chair of the MFA Design Department
at New York's School of Visual Arts. He is the author
of over 130 books on graphic design and popular culture,
most recently *Graphic*, *Handwritten*, *New Vintage Type*, and
New Ornamental Type, all published by Thames & Hudson.

Lita Talarico is co-chair of the MFA Design Department
at New York's School of Visual Arts; co-director of the SVA
Masters Workshop in Venice and Rome; formerly the founding
managing editor of *American Illustration & Photography*; and
a founding associate of Bill Lacy Design consulting firm.

Acknowledgments

The authors are indebted to Lucas Dietrich, our editor, for
his instrumental support for this project. Many thanks also
to Jennie Condell for her invaluable editorial supervision,
and Ashley Olsson, designer, for his talent and enthusiasm.

Tips of our well-worn hats to all the type designers,
typographers and designers who contributed so much
to this volume.

—SH + LT

First published in the United Kingdom in 2011 by
Thames & Hudson Ltd, 181A High Holborn,
London WC1V 7QX

Reprinted 2014

Typography Sketchbooks © 2011
Steven Heller & Lita Talarico

Extracts from sketchbooks © 2011
the designers and typographers

British Library Cataloguing-in-Publication Data

A catalogue record for this book is available
from the British Library

ISBN 978-0-500-24138-7 (hardback)

ISBN 978-0-500-28968-6 (paperback)

Printed and bound in China by
C&C Offset Printing Co. Ltd

To find out about all our publications, please visit
www.thamesandhudson.com. There you can subscribe
to our e-newsletter, browse or download our current
catalogue, and buy any titles that are in print.